JAMES JOYCE

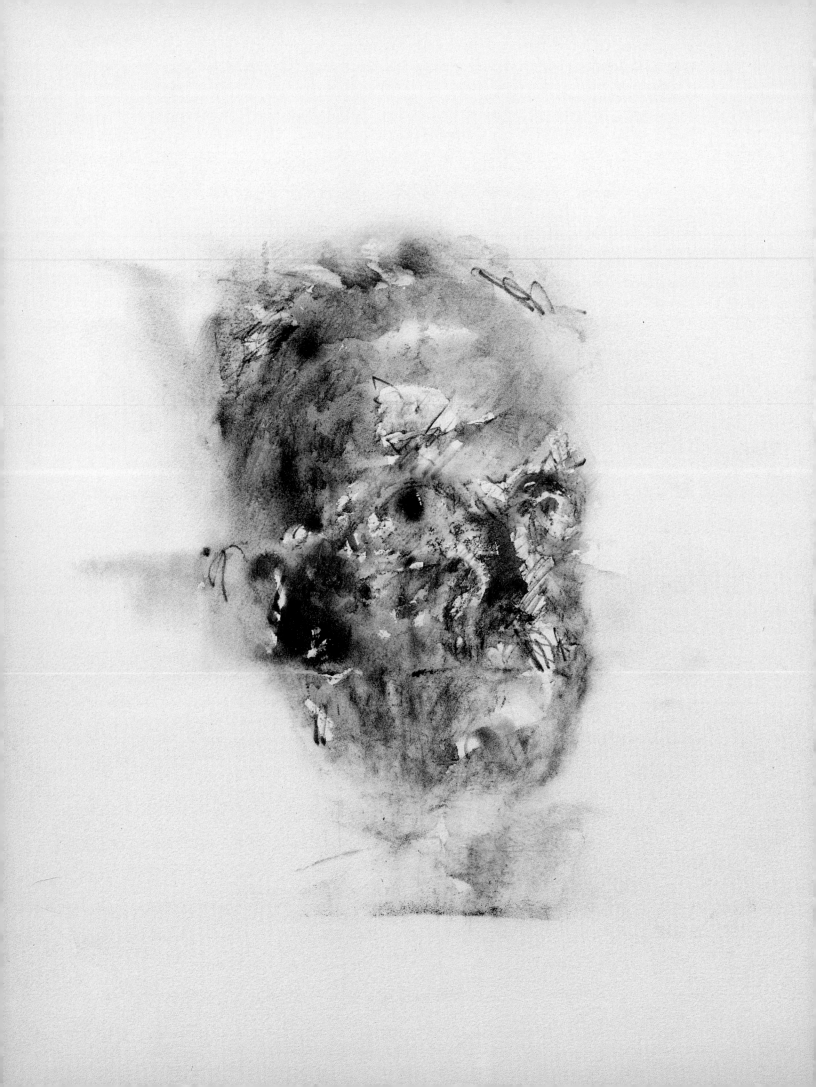

JAMES JOYCE

A PASSIONATE EXILE

John McCourt

Thomas Dunne Books

St Martin's Press ✹ New York

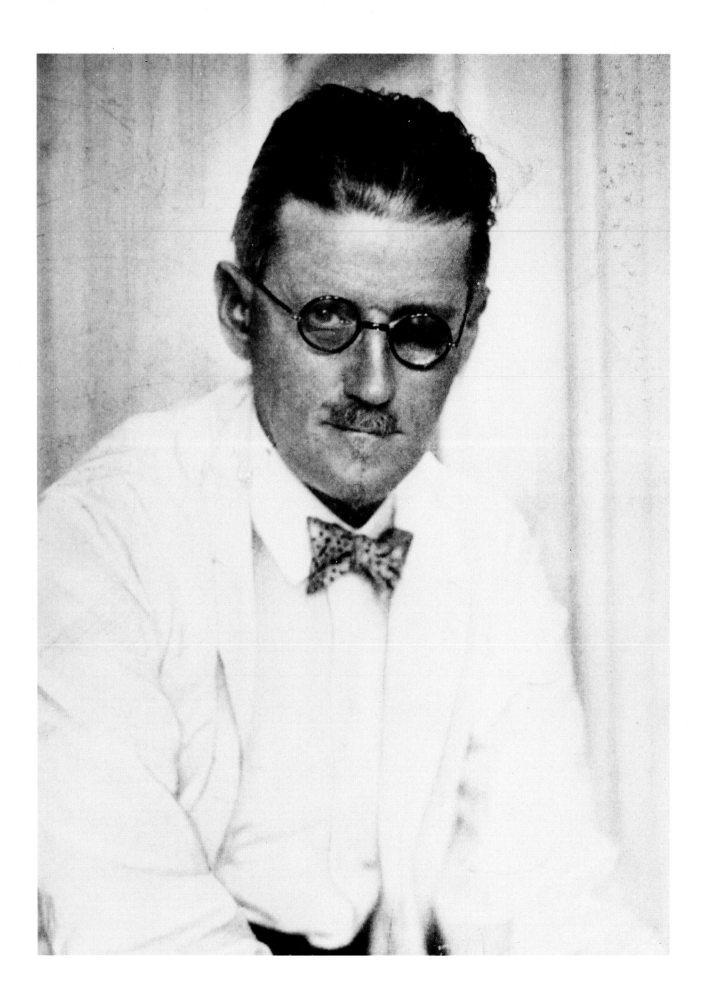

CONTENTS

To my parents James and Moira McCourt

FOREWORD

Several standard versions of Joyce's life are readily available and this short, illustrated life is but a swift gallop over familiar territory and is hugely dependent on all the previous biographies.

In Dublin I would like to thank Father Bruce Bradley S.J., who first introduced me to Joyce's *A Portrait of the Artist as a Young Man* at Belvedere College; Joyce's nephew, Ken Monaghan, who, over the course of many years, has taught me so much about Joyce's family; the late Augustine Martin of University College Dublin, who, more than anyone else, brought *Ulysses* and especially its abundant humour alive for me. I would also like to express my gratitude to Anthony Roche of UCD for his continuing encouragement and support.

In Trieste I owe a particular debt to Renzo Crivelli, Director of the Trieste Joyce School and of the Department of Anglo-Germanic Literature at the University of Trieste, where I currently work as a researcher; to Nick Carter, who patiently read and corrected the manuscript; and to my wife, Laura Pelaschiar, who read and corrected and improved practically every word I wrote.

I would also like to thank Fritz Senn of the Zurich James Joyce Foundation, who has been a loyal but challenging supporter over several years.

I also wish to express my thanks to Trevor Dolby and Pandora White of The Orion Publishing Group for their interest in this project, and to Tom Graves for doing such a wonderful job in the photo archives.

THOMAS DUNNE BOOKS
An imprint of St. Martin's Press

JAMES JOYCE: A PASSIONATE EXILE.
Copyright © 1999 by John McCourt. All rights reserved.
Printed in Italy. No part of this book may be used or reproduced
in any other mannerwhatsoever without written permission
except in the case of brief quotationsembodied in critical articles
or reviews, For information, address St. Martin's Press,
175 Fifth Avenue, New York, N.Y 10010.

ISBN 0-312-26941-2

First published in Great Britain by
Orion Media, an imprint of Orion Books Ltd.

Designed by Staziker Jones, Cardiff

First U.S. edition
10 9 8 7 6 5 4 3 2 1

Printed in Italy by Printer Trento S.r.l.

PICTURE CREDITS

Endpapers front and back
The Custom House, Dublin, on Joyce's beloved Liffey in the late
nineteenth century. *Hulton Getty*

Page 1. 'Agile and lean, his rigid legs like the poles of a compass, he
went about with an abstracted look. In summer he wore a Panama hat
of indescribable colour and old shoes' – Alessandro Francini Bruni in
his 1922 lecture on Joyce entitled *Joyce: Naked in the Market place*.
Cartoon by *Sergio Bon*.

Page 2. Image of James Joyce by Louis le Brocquy, 1983. Watercolour
61 x 46 cm, by kind permission of the artist.

Page 4. Joyce in the late 1920s. *State University of New York at Buffalo.*

INTRODUCTION

James Joyce placed himself and the events of his own life at the centre of practically everything he wrote. He claimed that he did so simply because he had little or no imagination. Whatever the truth of his view, Joyce's own life *is* the chief subject-matter of his writings, and his works do abound with versions of himself, which are never repetitive and are always revealing. Glancing through his stories and novels, we encounter the young Joyce in the sensitive little Dublin lad of the opening stories of *Dubliners* and in the Baby Tuckoo, who becomes Stephen Dedalus – young boy and adult – in *A Portrait of the Artist as a Young Man*. Later we meet more adult versions, such as Gabriel Conroy, the self-satisfied Dublin scribe in 'The Dead', whose view of his own marriage and his false life brings *Dubliners* to a close and who might well be read as Joyce's vision of what he would have become had he stayed in Dublin. A portrait of Joyce abroad is to be found in the voyeuristic, pleasure-tempted young Continental hero of the novelette *Giacomo Joyce*, struggling with his own sexuality and his attraction to a beautiful young Triestine girl. Joyce's most complete and sympathetic version of himself is not so much the Stephen Dedalus of *Ulysses* as his counter-character and father-figure, Leopold Bloom, the 'cultured alroundman', the endlessly curious, Europeanized Dublin hero of the book.

Joyce used everything he came into contact with as a possible source for his creative projects, but he gave particular importance to events involving his immediate circle – Nora, his family and his friends – in order to mould them into his writing. He sometimes went so far as to make things happen in real life so that he could later fictionalize them; he rarely seems to have worried about the possible consequences for those directly involved.

But Joyce also made Ireland – the country he left behind when he was just twenty-two, but whose imaginative clutches he never escaped – the pivotal point of his creative output. Although he spent his whole life writing about Dublin, he did so in the knowledge that he could not do so while living there and that he had to stand apart and embrace the life of an exile in order to be true to his mission to 'create at last a conscience in the soul of this wretched race'. Despite his melodramatic claim about having been driven out of his own country, it was the writer himself who initially barred his way to a future there, deciding to cast himself in the role of the exile in mainland Europe. The forced detachment from Dublin brought him into contact with a rich, cosmopolitan European world that furnished him with ideas and experiences on which he could draw in order to broaden and deepen his writings, to make Dublin a European centre, to universalize his own local world. It mattered little to him if the material he needed presented itself in Pola, Trieste, Rome, Zurich, Paris or anywhere else: he made it all fit into his own very particular Hibernian metropolis of Dublin.

He would later refer to himself in *Finnegans Wake* as 'self exiled in upon his own ego', and in this sense his exile was not simply physical removal from Ireland, but involved a sort of spiritual detachment from those around him in favour of a self-reliance which became stronger as his literary projects grew in ambition. It also involved a detachment from himself, which he needed in order to reinvent that very self in his auto-confessional stories and books. This is true in a very direct way not only of *A Portrait of the Artist as a Young Man*, *Exiles* and *Ulysses*, but also of *Finnegans Wake*, itself sometimes read as a form of confession or 'confussion' (to use one of its own terms) and yet another example of his fondness for what he described in *A Portrait of the Artist as a Young Man* as 'the joy of guilty confession'.

'Self' and 'exile' are key terms for any understanding of Joyce's enterprise. His various forms of exile did not simply express cold detachment, but rather a distrust of and a distaste for belonging, and a fear of conformity. At great personal cost he chose a harder path than that of the mediocrity of compromise and conformity, selecting instead a life of detachment which allowed only creative return to Ireland, with all the loneliness and loss that brought him. Yet his detachment was vital, it was the key condition for his writing. It was accompanied by a great hatred of, but also a passionate yearning for, that from which he lived apart – his country, his Church, his city, his language, the quotidian demands which cause normal everyday people to worry, and sometimes even his family – those very elements which form the body of his writings and which he used to become this century's most controversial, influential and celebrated writer.

Nelson's Pillar, a popular Dublin landmark, mentioned several times in Ulysses *and, in particular, in connection with the two elderly women who 'want to see the views of Dublin from the top of Nelson's Pillar' in the 'Aeolus' episode (painting by Leo Whelan, Bridgeman Art Library / Collection Earl of Mountcharles).*

1

'DEAR DIRTY DUBLIN'

On 2 February 1882 James Augustine Joyce was born the eldest son of John Stanislaus Joyce and Mary Jane (May) Murray, at 41 Brighton Square West in the pleasant, middle-class suburb of Rathgar in Dublin. He was the first son of an only son of an only son of an only son and very much the favourite of the ten children in his family. He had six sisters – Poppie, Eileen, May, Eva, Florrie and Baby, and three brothers – Stanislaus, Charles and George. In utterly contrasting ways, both parents loved him with extraordinary intensity and both were destined to leave lasting marks on Joyce – man and writer.

His father came from a well-off property-owning family in Cork and considered himself a gentleman, but showed precious little skill in preserving the sizeable inheritance which might have entitled him to such a status. Having failed to construct a worthwhile life in his native city, he moved to Dublin in his twenties and there embarked upon a rather uncertain career. In 1892 he lost the most stable and well-paid position he was ever to fill – that of rates collector for Dublin Corporation, which he had held for some ten years – blaming his dismissal on the political upheaval following the political demise of his hero, the great Irish leader Charles Stewart Parnell. In reality his own indolence, improvidence, aversion to hard work and fondness for drink were the principal ingredients of his downfall.

Although John Stanislaus was a difficult man, a bully, a typical example of that very Irish type the 'street-angel-house-devil', Joyce nearly always managed to get on with his father, despite their frequent misunderstandings, and later made him an essential presence in his writings. Stephen Dedalus's long catalogue of his father's occupations in *A Portrait of the Artist as a Young Man* – Joyce's highly stylized and sometimes wilfully inaccurate rendering of his own youth – owes much to John Stanislaus, who at one time or another filled most of the roles listed by Stephen: 'a medical

Cork city panorama by Nathaniel Grogan. Joyce's ancestors were prosperous and had property there, which Joyce's father sold off when times were bad (Bridgeman Art Library / Crawford Municipal Art Gallery, Cork).

The Joyce family — young James with his grandfather (left), May, his mother, and (right) his father (State University of New York at Buffalo).

student, an oarsman, a tenor, an amateur actor, a shouting politician, a small landlord, a small investor, a drinker, a good fellow, a storyteller, somebody's secretary, something in a distillery, a taxgatherer, a bankrupt and at present a praiser of his own past'. Of all the children, young James alone inherited his father's sense of entitlement and only he grew up to be fully able to forgive him his profligate ways and appreciate the aspects of his personality that led his friends and cronies to consider him 'a great character'. Following his death in 1931, Joyce wrote of his fondness for his father, who he considered a fellow sinner, even admitted to liking his faults and expressed his gratitude towards him for the role he played in his creative imagination, stating that 'hundreds of pages and scores of characters' came from him. Indeed John Stanislaus was Joyce's principal model for the character of Stephen Dedalus in *A Portrait of the Artist as a Young Man* and *Ulysses*, and for Earwicker in *Finnegans Wake*. Joyce famously told his Paris friend Louis Gillet that, although his father never said anything about his books, '...he couldn't deny me. The humour of *Ulysses* is his; its people are his friends. The book is his spittin' image.'

Joyce's mother's presence is much more shadowy. The daughter of a Dublin wines and spirits agent, May Murray married John Stanislaus Joyce in 1880, expecting to embark upon a comfortable middle-class existence with him. Little did she know that what awaited her would be a life of hardship as 'a selfish drunkard's unselfish wife', to quote her second son Stanislaus. She went through a total of fifteen pregnancies between 1881 and 1893, and suffered the agony of seeing five of her children die at birth or in early infancy. Especially after the family's fortunes went into decline in the 1890s, following her husband's loss of his job, she alone fought the battle to feed and clothe her family and attempted with increasing desperation to shield them from her husband's bitter and often drunken anger. She was selflessly devoted to her children and had a particularly close relationship with James, who she tried to support and understand in every way possible, even though his rejection of the Catholic Church, of which she was a devout member, caused her great pain. A moving letter she sent him in Paris in 1902 illustrates both her humility and her generosity towards him:

> My dear Jim if you are disappointed in my letter and if as usual I fail to understand what you would wish to explain, believe me it is not from any want of a longing desire to do so and speak the words you want but as you so often said I am stupid and cannot grasp the great thoughts which are yours much as I desire to do so.

At the young age of forty-three she was diagnosed as having cancer and died on 13 August 1903, leaving Joyce with an enormous sense of loss and guilt. Later, to Nora Barnacle, he movingly described the financial ruin in which his mother's death took place, claiming that she was killed slowly by her brave but endless struggle to look after her family, by his father's ill-treatment of her and by his own 'cynical frankness of conduct'.

But things were not so grim in 1882, the year in which Joyce was born. His father had just been taken on by Dublin Corporation, the family was ensconced in respectable Brighton Terrace and Joyce's first memories of his childhood are happy ones. This atmosphere is mirrored in the opening lines of *A Portrait of the Artist as a Young Man*, where Stephen's first recollection is a pleasant one of his father telling him stories:

Once upon a time and a very good time it was there was a moocow coming down along the road and this moocow that was coming down along the road met a nicens little boy named baby tuckoo....

His father told him that story: his father looked at him through a glass: he had a hairy face.

He was baby tuckoo.

What young James and his increasingly numerous siblings did not yet know was that their apparently comfortable and prosperous world was built on perilously shaky financial foundations. With his notions of grandeur, his father was unwilling or unable to live within the limits of his not inconsiderable salary. He fell increasingly into debt by taking out several ill-advised mortgages on the properties he had inherited in Cork in order to move his family firstly to a better, three-storey house at 23 Castlewood Avenue in the nearby suburb of Rathmines, and subsequently, in 1887, to an impressive house at 1 Martello Terrace in Bray, a seaside suburb south of Dublin. In 1888 he took on a further weighty financial commitment when he decided to send his son James away to boarding school at the expensive Clongowes Wood College in County Kildare, then, as now, one of Ireland's foremost

Thomas Moore (1779–1852) wrote 124 Irish melodies (mostly patriotic ballads), which were still hugely popular in the Ireland of Joyce's youth. He would often have heard his father sing them at home and enjoyed singing them himself. Practically all the melodies are referred to in Finnegans Wake *and the famous 'Oft in the Stilly Night' is included in* A Portrait of the Artist as a Young Man *(Weidenfeld Archive).*

educational establishments, founded by the Society of Jesus primarily to provide young Catholics with an education which would prepare them to take up positions in the professions.

Six-and-a-half-year-old James (seated front) at Clongowes Wood College. He was the youngest boy at the school (Father Bruce Bradley SJ).

At the astonishingly young age of just six and a half, after a journey of some thirty miles by train and jaunting car, Joyce passed through the imposing gates and up the long, impressive tree-lined avenue to begin his studies at Clongowes Wood College. Probably the youngest child ever to enter this school, he was beginning what in a sense was his first exile from home and family. While this undoubtedly did help mould that extraordinary independence which would become one of the defining characteristics of his personality, it must also have been a daunting and at times traumatic experience for him. Joyce remained in the hands of the Jesuits for a further fifteen years until he graduated from University College Dublin in 1902, and he later attached great importance to these years, which he had his first biographer, Herbert Gorman, describe as 'the novitiate, the preparatory training for all that was to follow'.

The school was presided over by Father John Conmee SJ – 'the decentest rector that was ever in Clongowes', according to Stephen Dedalus – and by the rather cruel Dean of Studies, Father James Daly, the 'Baldyhead Dolan' of *A Portrait of the Artist as a Young Man*, who pandies Stephen after wrongly accusing him of being a 'lazy little schemer' and of breaking his glasses in order to escape doing his school work. No record of this event survives, although Joyce was punished several times for misbehaving. One such punishment occurred on 14 March 1889, when the seven-year-old was sent to the Prefect of Studies for using 'vulgar language', as the *Punishment Book* records it.

Joyce took his place in the Elements class with some forty other boys – all at least two years older than he – and because of his tender age remained in that class for most of his three years in the college. For the most part his time in Clongowes was reasonably happy, although he did suffer from loneliness and was the victim of occasional bullying. Accustomed to thinking of his father as a 'gentleman', Joyce also began to be troubled by his uncertain place in the world and to realize that something more specific was needed if he were to keep up with his classmates, most of whom seemed to be the sons of 'magistrates'. The temporary strategy Joyce ascribes to Stephen Dedalus – to lie and claim that he had 'an uncle a judge and an uncle a general in the army' – may well have been the one he himself employed.

It was in Clongowes that a religious dimension in Joyce's life began to form. He describes this process happening to Stephen Dedalus, beginning with the very young Dedalus's early childlike sense of God:

From the age of six and a half until he graduated from University College Dublin sixteen years later, Joyce was moulded by the Jesuits (State University of New York at Buffalo).

It was very big to think about everything and everywhere. Only God could do that. He tried to think what a big thought that must be but he could think only of God. God was God's name just as his name was Stephen. *Dieu* was the French for God and that was God's name too; and when anyone prayed to God and said Dieu then God knew at once that it was a French person that was praying. But though there were different names for God in all the different languages in the world and God understood what all the people who prayed said in their different languages still God remained always the same God and God's real name was God.

It made him very tired to think that way.

A regulated life of silence, prayer, sacraments, Mass, retreats, devotions and religious education both in Clongowes and later in Belvedere left its mark: Joyce became so earnestly devout that he was chosen to be an altar boy, a task he performed enthusiastically. He also developed a fondness for the liturgy of the Mass and for Church music, which he would retain throughout his life.

Charles Stewart Parnell (1846–1891), the uncrowned king of Ireland. His fall from grace was regarded by the Joyce family as Ireland's greatest tragedy and Joyce later celebrated him in his short story 'Ivy Day in the Committee Room' (Bridgeman Art Library / Private Collection).

While he was busily occupied at school, life in the Joyce home did not get any easier. In a seemingly endless succession of births and mortgages, the family grew larger and poorer, and to try to make ends meet Joyce's father continued to sell off more of his Cork properties. Joyce senior's sense of betrayal and of failure was compounded by what was happening to Ireland in general, and in particular by the spectacular fall of the great Irish leader – the uncrowned king, Charles Stewart Parnell. As the Christmas Dinner scene in *A Portrait of the Artist as a Young Man*

'Dear Dirty Dublin': two turn-of-the-century views of the city centre. Joyce liked to claim that he had a family connection with Daniel O'Connell, the Great Liberator, whose statue stands in front of Nelson's Pillar (middle ground, above) in what was then called Sackville Street (now O'Connell Street). (Below) The trams, now long gone, were a potent feature of city life and a prominent presence in Ulysses *(both Hulton Getty).*

shows so clearly, even though the country was bitterly divided with regard to Parnell, a sense of loss, of lost possibility, of betrayal and powerlessness was deeply felt by everyone. At just nine years of age, in his poem 'Et Tu Healy', which was partly inspired by his father, Joyce was already registering these sentiments and attacking Timothy Healy, Parnell's foremost accuser within the Irish Home Rule Party, of which he was leader. Later, to his friends and in his writings, Joyce liked to compare Parnell to Moses, a great leader who brought his people to within sight of the promised land in almost achieving Irish Home Rule, and he never forgave his narrow-minded fellow Irishmen for betraying their leader in his moment of greatest need.

In November 1891 Joyce's sojourn at Clongowes was brought to an abrupt and unceremonious conclusion when his family could no longer afford the rather expensive fees and had to withdraw him. They were also forced to move to a slightly more modest house on Carysfort Avenue in Blackrock, a south Dublin suburb. While his brothers and sisters attended a local convent, Joyce received no formal education in this period and was largely left to his own devices. Worse was to come. In the summer of 1892 John Stanislaus Joyce was suspended from his job, because news of his indebtedness had become public, and soon he was forced to retire on a pension which was just one-third of his salary. The family had no choice but to move again, this time into a big, unfurnished and cheerless house at 14 Fitzgibbon Street in the run-down north inner city.

This was to be their first major step downward in the world, the beginning of their harsh and inexorable fall from middle-class respectability. Having known comfort and security, the Joyces were suddenly faced with hardship and loss of face, and would soon encounter real poverty: theirs would be, as Stanislaus put it, the 'house of the bare table'. Yet hard though this new reality must have been for the impressionable ten-year-old Joyce, it was in many respects the making of him as a writer. It brought him into 'the heart of the Hibernian metropolis' he was later to present to the world, to the centre of a Dublin he would make his own and which would never cease to dominate his

creative consciousness. Because he came to know at first hand what it meant to live on so many of the rungs of the social ladder, to tumble unceremoniously from a refined south Dublin suburb to a dingy house on a dull brown street across the River Liffey in north central Dublin, more than any other Irish writer before him Joyce became sensitive to the power of money or its lack, to questions and nuances of class and the petty cruelties involved in claiming one's place. Using his style of 'scrupulous meanness', drawing from what he saw of his new down-at-heel, lower-middle-class neighbours and absorbing the atmosphere and odours of the narrow mean streets which were now his home, Joyce was able to create an astonishingly authentic range of characters for *Dubliners* and to imbue his Dublin with a crippling atmosphere of endless struggle in a world of spiritual and economic deprivation.

Despite his family's fall, Joyce's expectations and world view remained substantially middle class; he managed to maintain a tenuous foothold in bourgeois society through some friends, such as the Sheehys, a prominent, successful legal family who offered him a glimpse of a world that might have been his by having him take part in the dancing, recitations, charades and singing, as well as the lively discussions which took place during the Sunday evening entertainments in their home. Later, in Trieste, although the common image of him was that of a penniless teacher, Joyce still managed to give the impression that he came from a moneyed Dublin family, so much so that Almidano Artifoni, the owner of the Berlitz school, nurtured hopes of being able to sell the school to his Irish employee.

Shortly after the family's arrival north of the Liffey, Joyce enrolled in the local Christian Brothers' school on North Richmond Street, where he studied for a couple of months along with his brother Stanislaus. This happening is only briefly aired in *A Portrait of the Artist as a Young Man*, where Stephen Dedalus rejects it angrily: 'Christian brothers be damned! said Mr Dedalus. Is it with Paddy Stink and Micky Mud? No, let him stick to the jesuits in God's name since he began with them.'

In the spring of 1893 Father John Conmee kindly offered James and Stanislaus a free education at Belvedere College, and Joyce's father was quick to accept, happy to send his sons back to the Jesuits and to one of Ireland's premier day-schools for boys. Belvedere was located in a fine Georgian house on Great Denmark Street in central Dublin, where it had been functioning as a Jesuit school since 1841. The Joyce brothers immediately settled down to life there and performed well academically, being taught by a string of competent teachers, both Jesuit and lay.

Opposite above:
The Wellington Monument in Phoenix Park, commemorating Arthur Wellesley, later Duke of Wellington and hero of the Battle of Waterloo, makes regular appearances in Finnegans Wake *as the 'Willingdone Museyroom' (Hulton Getty).*

Opposite below: Howth c.1900, a seaside town north of Dublin, is referred to in the opening lines of Finnegans Wake *and figures prominently in* Ulysses, *for it is there that Leopold Bloom first kisses Molly and later proposes to her (Hulton Getty).*

Joyce in costume in the Belvedere school performance of Vice-Versa *aged 15 in 1895 (Father Bruce Bradley SJ).*

The most influential for Joyce was Mr George Dempsey, a widely read and challenging teacher of English (remembered as Mr Tate in *A Portrait of the Artist as a Young Man*), who immediately realized that he had in James a very special student and allowed him free rein to develop his essay-writing skills.

Despite continuing difficulties at home – in 1893 John Stanislaus was forced to sell off what little remained of his Cork properties in order to pay his debts – Joyce was clearly a leader in his class at Belvedere and took part in a full range of curricular and extra-curricular activities. He acted in a play entitled 'Vice-Versa', doing a brilliant imitation of the rector of the school Father Henry, he won a number of lucrative public examination prizes and, in 1895, he was elected a member of the Sodality of the Blessed Virgin. Two years later he became Prefect of the Sodality, a position which made him head of the school in all but name. Through reflection on Catholic texts and prayerful devotion to the Blessed Virgin, this Sodality attempted to instil high ideals plus strong Christian faith and morals in the boys who were its members and who were of an age at which they were in danger of falling prey to dangerous temptations.

To the Jesuits Joyce appeared to be ideal sodality material, but what they did not know was that their model pupil was already leading something of a double life, having yielded to the temptations of prostitutes who worked but a stone's throw from the school gates. In *A Portrait of the Artist as a Young Man,* Joyce describes Stephen surrendering himself physically to these prostitutes in a 'swoon of sin' which returns to haunt him in the days and weeks following his visits. Indeed, one of the main confessional dynamics of the book is Stephen's coming to terms with his own sexuality, which initially is seen only in terms of sinfulness before it is gradually allowed to become an integral part of his artistic personality, a necessary freedom. Stephen is racked with guilt for having 'sinned mortally not once but many times' and frightened of the consequences, realizing that he 'stood in danger of eternal damnation'. There is every reason to believe that Joyce shared such fears and, although he would soon formally reject the Church, he would never entirely liberate himself from this complex nexus of Catholic sexual guilt. His mother's pious Catholicism played an important part in initiating it; the religious education he received at Belvedere and especially the sermons of the annual retreat there

Joyce lovingly describes seeing pretty girls walking on such a Dublin beach (painting by Heywood Hardy, Bridgeman Art Library / Julian Simon Fine Art Ltd, London).

deepened it further and his own spiralling imagination did the rest. In *A Portrait of the Artist as a Young Man* these sermons, delivered by a certain Father Arnall, who draws on Giovanni Pietro Pinamonti's seventeenth-century 'Hell Opened to Christians, To Caution Them from Entering It', were terrifying triumphs of rhetoric and style on the themes of sin, punishment and eternal damnation.

The brimstone too which burns there in such prodigious quantity fills all hell with its intolerable stench; and the bodies of the damned themselves exhale such a pestilential odour that as saint Bonaventure says, one of them alone would suffice to infect the whole world.

John Pentland Mahaffey (1839–1919), classical scholar and long-time Provost of Trinity College. Of the founding of University College, Dublin, he later said: 'James Joyce is a living argument in favour of my contention that it was a mistake to establish a separate university for the aborigines of this island – for the corner-boys who spit into the Liffey' (Hulton Getty).

While such overcharged diatribes might easily have been forgotten or dismissed by the other boys with cleaner consciences, they aroused huge emotional and religious turmoil in Stephen, who soon went to confession and set about mending his ways, undertaking to lead a life of contrition and religious fervour which lasted several months. Indeed, such was his piety that the Jesuit Director summoned him to his office and suggested he might have a vocation:

> In a college like this, he said at length, there is one boy or perhaps two or three boys whom God calls to the religious life. Such a boy is marked off from his companions by his piety, by the good example he shows to others … Perhaps you are the boy in this college whom God designs to call to Himself.

Joyce, too, was such a boy, and all these events were experienced with greater or lesser intensity by him, including the religious calling to which he gave very serious consideration before ultimately rejecting it. Later in *Finnegans Wake*, he would poke fun at his own youthful piety and his hope that 'the rowmish devowtion known as the howly rowsary might reeform ihm'. In *A Portrait* the rejection comes as Stephen walks along Dollymount Strand, where his desire to see the world and his lust for freedom, develop into a mystical experience which causes him to reject the priest's life of self-control and abnegation in order to embrace life itself and fulfil his desire to encounter the world in all its manifold forms. Not willing to accept the constraints of a celibate life, Stephen chooses to follow his own 'wayward instinct', which is brought alive by the vision of a girl who walks before him along the strand and awakens his sexual desires, giving him a new sense of life, a new sense of his true artistic mission.

Although Joyce's vocation was ultimately to be artistic and not religious, he did gratefully avail himself of religious terminology and symbolism to describe this aesthetic enterprise. He sought to confer upon himself

an almost sacred role, to construct a 'priesthood of art' that would be capable of elevating or rather of transubstantiating the quotidian into a thing of permanance and beauty. This quasi-religious artistic enterprise was steeped in the teachings of Aristotle and Aquinas, and its hallmarks were *integritas* (wholeness), *consonantia* (symmetry) and, above all, *claritas* (radiance). Through this aesthetic he would exhalt both sublime and vulgar reality, make it holy and render life in all its beauty as well as in all its ugliness, artistically appealing.

In 1898 Joyce enrolled in University College Dublin, which had been founded by Cardinal John Henry Newman in 1853 as the Catholic University, and which was situated at 85 and 86 St Stephen's Green. A rather desultory student, he was somewhat resentful of the overbearing Catholic and nationalistic ethos of the University and its three hundred students. As he put it in *Stephen Hero* (as he called an early draft of *A Portrait of the Artist as a Young Man*): 'The deadly chill of the atmosphere of the college paralysed Stephen's heart. In a stupor of powerlessness he reviewed the plague of Catholicism.' Joyce chose to study modern languages – French, Italian and English – and, although he showed only relative interest in his official courses, he still formed worthwhile intellectual relationships with his mother-tongue teachers of French and Italian, Edouard Cadic and Father Charles Ghezzi. Ghezzi, in particular, gave his pupil a firm grounding in Italian language and literature, and helped him come to terms with writers who were to be palpable presences in his writing, such as Dante, D'Annunzio, Cavalcanti and the philosopher Giordano Bruno. Their exchange over Bruno became famous, because when Ghezzi

Henrik Ibsen (1828–1906). Following Joyce's favourable review of Ibsen's When We Dead Awaken, *Ibsen asked his translator William Archer to thank 'Mr James Joyce (for his) very benevolent review' (painting by E. T. Werenskiold, Bridgeman Art Library / Nasjonalgalleriet, Oslo).*
© DACS, 2000

*Title page of Joyce's
published essay on Ibsen
(Weidenfeld Archive).*

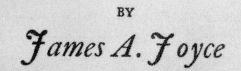

Ibsen's New Drama

[From *The Fortnightly Review* LONDON April 1900].

BY

James A. Joyce

ULYSSES BOOKSHOP
187, High Holborn, London, W. C. 4

pointed out that Bruno had been a terrible heretic, Joyce coolly retorted: 'Yes, and he was terribly burned.'

Joyce's reading at university was prolific and he spent much time in the National Library in Kildare Street devouring the classics of English and European literature. Although somewhat aloof from his fellow students, he had quite a circle of talented, opinionated and ambitious companions: John Francis Byrne (Cranly in *A Portrait of the Artist as a Young Man*), his closest college friend; Thomas Kettle, as outspokenly European as Joyce himself, later elected a Member of Parliament and killed fighting in the British army in 1916; Constantine Curran, editor of the college newspaper, *St Stephen's*, and an intellectual match for Joyce despite his piety; Vincent Cosgrave, a coarse-spoken yet witty companion and Francis Skeffington (McCann in *A Portrait of the Artist as a Young Man*), in Joyce's opinion the most intelligent man in college after himself, a pacifist and feminist who was murdered in 1916 by a British officer later judged insane.

Joyce took an active and prominent part in college life and especially in the debates organised by the Literary and Historical Society. He contributed regularly to its weekly sessions, was elected to its executive committee and never lost his reputation for his singular, forthright and often idiosyncratic views. Of particular note was his 1899 address 'Drama and Life', in which he distinguished between drama and literature, praised Ibsen at the expense of Shakespeare and, after being roundly attacked from the floor, defended himself so masterfully that at the close he was told by a colleague: 'Joyce, that was magnificent, but you're raving mad.' It would not be the last time he had to listen to such sentiments. Soon afterwards, to the envious astonishment of his companions, Joyce was vindicated when the prestigious *Fortnightly Review* published his review of Ibsen's *When We Dead Awaken*, entitled 'Ibsen's New Drama'. A few weeks later he received a letter from Ibsen's translator, William Archer, telling him that Ibsen had asked him to thank 'Mr James Joyce' for his 'very benevolent review'. Joyce was thrilled and immediately replied with rare candour: 'I am a young Irishman, eighteen years old, and the words of Ibsen I shall keep in my heart all my life.'

While his colleagues used their university years to prepare themselves to take up positions of responsibility in the new Ireland, Joyce began consciously to forge a role for himself as an artist who would undermine most of their assumptions about what that Ireland should be like. In these years he began to develop that astounding sense of mission which allowed him to serve his art at the expense of all else and which was described by Stanislaus as his 'proud, wilful, vicious selfishness … [and] extraordinary moral courage'. Stannie greatly aided and encouraged him in this, recognizing very early on that his brother's talent was exceptional.

Between 1900 and 1904, although Joyce was without a clear project into which he could plough his literary energies, he still wrote some seventy epiphanies, which he would later draw on as source materials for his novels, and his determination to become a writer was becoming stronger and more focused. His initial interest was in the theatre, and his biggest influence was Ibsen, whose writings he read in the original Dano-Norwegian and who he admired for his courage in dealing with hitherto unexplored themes, for his foregrounding of women characters, and for his having emerged from a small country with a minority language to become one of Europe's greatest playwrights. His interest did not stop with Ibsen, however, and in 1900 he was pleased to travel to London to see the renowned Italian actress Eleonora Duse star in *La Gioconda*, using this visit to renew his acquaintance with William Archer. In May of the same year he sent his first play, *My Brilliant Career*, to Archer, who rejected it. He spent the following summer with his father, who was working in Mullingar, and translated Gerhart

William Butler Yeats (1865–1939), Ireland's great poet, was already a major literary figure by the time Joyce was establishing himself as a writer in Dublin. They first met in 1902 and on several occasions Joyce was generously helped by the older man, whose genius he always acknowledged publicly no matter how deep his reservations about Yeats's Irish Literary Revival (Weidenfeld Archive).

Hauptmann's *Michael Kramer* and his *Vor Sonnenaufgang*. In 1901 he published a pamphlet, entitled 'The Day of the Rabblement', at his own expense after the college censor had refused to allow it to appear in the student paper, *St Stephen's*. It attacked the timid insularity of the Irish theatre for its refusal to accept the influence of contemporary European drama and created the kind of stir Joyce needed in order to establish his reputation as an independent-minded young intellectual.

The following autumn Joyce sat his final examinations at University College Dublin and, although both he and his family were disappointed with his mediocre results (he was to be the only one the family could afford to send to university), his father insisted that he have his photograph taken in cap and gown. After graduation, despite his decision to embark upon the study of medicine, Joyce took up a rather aimless, Bohemian way of life; he had no genuine interest in medical subjects, his family was in no position to keep him financially and the university was unable to offer him work as a tutor. Meanwhile he continued to write and established acquaintances with the leading literary lights of the Irish revival whom he so publicly disdained, such as Lady Gregory, George Russell ('A.E.') and W. B. Yeats. Russell was immediately impressed by him and told Yeats: 'The first spectre of the new generation has appeared. His name is Joyce.' Soon Yeats agreed to meet Joyce, who, on hearing of the pre-eminent Irish poet's plans for his new work, told him: 'We have met too late. You are too old for me to have any effect on you.' Luckily Yeats was more amused than offended by this young pretender and asked him to write a play for the Irish Literary Theatre.

It was around this time that Joyce came up with the idea of pursuing his medical studies in Paris, at the Sorbonne. How he intended to finance this enterprise remains unclear, although he did plan to give English lessons, and E. V. Longworth of Dublin's *Daily Express* agreed to have him write reviews. Oblivious to the efforts of William Archer and others to dissuade him, Joyce managed to muster moral and financial

James Joyce, aged 22, every inch 'the young man about town', 1904 (State University of New York at Buffalo).

support from his father, Russell, Lady Gregory and Yeats, and thus departed on 1 December 1902.

His real agenda was a literary one. He found little in the contemporary Irish literary scene to inspire him and longed to explore the panorama of European modernism at first hand. As he put it in 'The Day of the Rabblement': 'A nation which never advanced so far as a miracle play affords no literary model to the artist, and he must look abroad'; and later in *Finnegans Wake* he asserted that 'he would far sooner muddle through the hash of lentils in Europe than meddle with Ireland's split little pea'. While it was true that Ireland boasted a surprisingly rich array of illustrious contemporary writers from Wilde to Yeats and Moore to Shaw, it was also true that they all pertained to different worlds from Joyce. Besides, a writer of his enormous ambition was never going to accept the constraints and the politics of the Irish Literary Revival or consciously to follow the footsteps of an Irish predecessor or contemporary. Likewise he was also anxious to avoid following the tradition by which an Irish writer usually sought to make his name in London, and so he chose to cast his nets wider. Like Stephen Dedalus, he needed space and time – silence, exile, cunning – in order to fly the nets of 'nationality, language, religion' and forge in the smithy of his soul the uncreated conscience of his race.

En route to Paris, Joyce stopped briefly in London, where Yeats bought him breakfast, lunch and dinner, and introduced him to a host of literary figures including Arthur Symons, the English advocate of the French symbolist movement. Having come to the conclusion that Joyce was 'a curious mixture of sinister genius and uncertain talent', Symons suggested that he should write articles on French literature for English journals. More importantly, he promised to help have Joyce's poems published and was to prove as good as his word.

Joyce arrived in Paris full of enthusiasm, preferring to enjoy his new writerly pose in this great Bohemian city of art rather than seriously weigh up the financial difficulties of maintaining himself there. He checked into the cheap but central Hotel Corneille and would spend his entire Paris sojourn there. He managed to get provisionally admitted to medical school before dropping out rapidly on discovering that his French was not of a standard to enable him to follow the lessons with ease and, more importantly, that the university expected him to pay his fees immediately, something he was patently incapable of doing. Joyce spent his time writing the odd review for the *Daily Express*, giving occasional private lessons, hanging

The world famous Irish born tenor John McCormack, who shared the stage in Dublin with Joyce in 1904 and later became his friend. He is pictured here with the painter Sir William Orpen (Hulton Getty).

about, soaking up the atmosphere of Paris and reading voraciously.

Money remained a major concern. Just two weeks after his departure from Dublin he wrote to his mother in mid-December tentatively suggesting that he might bring his much-announced exile to an abrupt if temporary end for the holiday season. His parents took out a further mortgage and sent a small part of it to Joyce to enable him to travel home for Christmas. Before leaving the French capital he had his photograph taken in a professional studio and visited a brothel so that he could, with at least some justification, brag to his friend Cosgrave, in a postcard written in dog Latin, about his immoral and Bohemian lifestyle.

After his month-long Christmas holiday, he returned to Paris, where he spent his days at the Bibliothèque Nationale and his evenings at the Bibliothèque Sainte-Geneviève, reading and writing occasional journalism and some poetry. Making ends meet continued to be a struggle and so he penned pathetic begging letters home demanding assistance, such as the following one of 8 March 1903:

> …My next meal therefore will be at 11 a.m. tomorrow (Monday): my last meal was 7 p.m. last (Saturday) night. So I have another fast of 40 hours – No, not a fast, for I have eaten a pennyworth of dry bread. My second last meal was 20 hours before my last. 20 and 40 = 60 – Two meals in 60 hours is not bad, I think.

Invariably his mother was moved to scrape together some money to send her son and sometimes, in order to do so, she pawned some jewellery or furniture. Joyce gratefully received whatever was sent and dined out in style for as long as it lasted, before plunging back into penury and starvation until the next instalment arrived.

Joyce formed several acquaintances with other expatriates during this period, including the Triestine-born German writer Teodor Daubler and the Fenian Joseph Casey, now a typesetter for the *New York Tribune* of Paris, who Joyce would restyle as Kevin Egan in *Ulysses*. On 6 March the Irish dramatist J. M. Synge arrived, and the two young writers spent a lot of time together. On being given a manuscript version of Synge's one-act tragedy *Riders to the Sea*, Joyce dismissed it to the author as mere 'dwarf-drama', although he would later publicly express his admiration for this and other of Synge's plays and chose it for the English Players Theatre

John Millington Synge (1871–1909) was greatly admired by Joyce. He wrote, among other masterpieces, The Playboy of the Western World *(1904) and* Riders to the Sea *(1907). The first production of* The Playboy *in the Abbey Theatre was greeted by a week of riots (Weidenfeld Archive).*

*Joyce's father, John Stanislaus, in a painting by Patrick Tuohy. It hung in
James Joyce's Paris apartment (State University of New York at Buffalo).*

Company, which he helped run in Zurich during the First World War. For his part, Synge noted that Joyce was 'pretty badly off', 'wandering around Paris rather unbrushed and rather indolent', but ultimately felt that 'his time in Paris is not wasted'.

On 10 April 1903 his Paris sojourn was brought to a sudden end when he received a telegram from his father, which read starkly: 'Mother dying come home Father'. He borrowed the price of his passage home and departed the following morning. Back in Dublin he was distressed at his mother's poorly state, but there was little he could do to comfort her, especially as he was unwilling to grant her wish to see him reconciled with the Church before her death, which came after an agonizing battle against cancer on 13 August 1903.

May Murray's premature death was a catastrophe for the Joyces. Without her the household simply began to break apart. John Stanislaus did not know where to turn for money, having squandered what was left of his commuted pension, and bit by bit he sold off whatever furniture remained in the house. Often there was no food to eat and the eldest girl, Poppie, who had pledged to her mother to look after the younger ones, struggled to find the means to do so. The father was increasingly rough and turned his anger particularly on his younger daughters, who he referred to as 'an insolent pack of little bitches'. Things were so bad at home that Joyce spent as little time as possible there, choosing to live with friends and relations or even in boarding houses.

For the moment he felt disinclined to return to Paris, preferring to drift around Dublin for the best part of eighteen months, living from hand to mouth, writing occasional reviews and making a half-hearted attempt to found a literary newspaper. He turned down the possibility of part-time teaching at University College Dublin in order to pursue 'the career of letters' and apparently felt under no obligation to find a job in order to help keep the younger members of the family, although he did work as a teacher for a short time in the Clifton School in Dalkey in the early autumn of 1904 (and would draw on this experience later for the 'Nestor' episode of *Ulysses*). He had also acquired the habit of drinking heavily, partly under the influence of his new friend/rival, the Oxford-educated Irish doctor, part-time poet and caustically witty man-about-town, Oliver St John Gogarty. In September 1904 he went to spend a few nights with Gogarty in the Martello tower the latter had rented in Sandycove. The tower would become the location of the opening 'Telemachus' episode of *Ulysses*, where Gogarty appears in the uncomplimentary and probably unfair guise of 'stately, plump Buck Mulligan', Dedalus's false friend. Joyce's stay in the tower was soured by the presence of a third party, the Anglo-Irish Charles Chevenix Trench (Haines in *Ulysses*), a former Oxford colleague of Gogarty's who was intent on discovering the 'real Ireland'. On the night of 14 September Joyce was awoken by the sound of Trench, his room-mate, screaming in his sleep about a black panther which was about to attack him. Joyce watched in amazement as Trench reached for his revolver and fired it a couple of times before going back to sleep. Soon Trench began screaming again and this time Gogarty intervened, taking the revolver and shooting at the pots hanging over Joyce's bed. Frightened, but even more furious, Joyce stormed out of the tower in the middle of

the night, never to return, convinced that it had all been a plot on Gogarty's part to get rid of him.

If, on the one hand, 1904 represented a low ebb in Joyce's Dublin life, on the other it was also destined to be the year that would change his life for the better. The first positive note came in an unfamiliar field – the musical one – when Joyce decided to have his sweet if slightly weak tenor voice trained in order to establish himself as a professional singer. He took singing lessons with the Italian maestro Benedetto Palmieri and soon was ready to take part in Ireland's most important singing competition, the *Feis Ceol*. He made a positive impression and would have been awarded the gold medal by the distinguished judge Professor Luigi Denza, the Italian

*Martello tower, Sandycove,
one of numerous
fortifications built by the
British at the start of the
nineteenth century to protect
Ireland from invasion by the
French. Joyce was the guest
of Oliver St John Gogarty in
the tower for a couple of
nights in September 1904
and later set the Telemachus
episode of* Ulysses *there
with Gogarty recast as Buck
Mulligan. The tower now
houses the James Joyce
Museum (Hulton Getty).*

composer of 'Funiculi-Funiculà', had he been willing or able to do a sight-reading test. Nevertheless, he still managed to win a bronze medal because of the excellence of his singing of the set pieces and secured several engagements on the strength of it.

Joyce's writing career also began to take direction. He wrote a short story entitled 'A Portrait of the Artist as a Young Man' for a literary magazine called *Dana* and, although rejected, this would become the basis for his more famous novel of the same name. He worked regularly now on this novel, although for the moment it was called *Stephen Hero*, the title suggested for it by Stannie. In the meantime George Russell asked him to write a story for *The Irish Homestead* and offered him a welcome fee of a pound for his trouble. Signing himself 'Stephen Daedalus', Joyce penned 'The Sisters', the story with which he would later choose to open *Dubliners* and which sets the tone for the whole collection with its study of physical and psychological paralysis, spiritual corruption and death. It was the first of three stories he published in *The Irish Homestead*, which he referred to as 'the pig's paper' because of its link with the Irish Agricultural Co-operative movement, the others being 'Eveline' (September 1904) and 'After the Race' (December 1904). Thus, by the second half of 1904, the two creative projects which would dominate Joyce's creative energies for the coming years – *A Portrait of the Artist as a Young Man* and *Dubliners*, his 'chapter in the moral history' of his country – were in train.

In August, Joyce's university friend Curran asked him to contribute again to *St Stephen's* magazine and, though he knew Joyce well, he must have been shocked to read the text of his offering, which took its title 'The Holy Office' from the sixteenth-century Church body established as part of the Counter-Reformation. It was a satirical poem in which Joyce, calling himself 'Katharsis-Purgative', rejected the Irish Literary Revival and its leading writers, many of them his contemporaries, and effectively announced his intention to plot what he considered to be his own more honest literary course. It was as if he were consciously seeking to alienate himself, passionately set himself apart in exile from all his Irish fellow writers, drive a wedge between himself and those who had sought to help him – Yeats, Synge, Russell, Gregory – and, so in doing, to leave himself no real possibility of succeeding as a writer in Dublin. In this way exile would become a necessary condition for his literary career – to be true to his artistic calling he would have no choice but to stand, as the poem puts it, 'unfellowed, friendless and alone'.

There was, however, another more pressing reason why he felt he had to flee

Left: Nora Barnacle
(State University of New York
at Buffalo).

Dublin. Her name was Nora Barnacle. He met her by chance in Dublin's Nassau Street for the first time on 10 June 1904, and she was to change his life utterly. A Galway girl who had finished her formal education at the age of twelve, Nora worked as a chambermaid in Finn's Hotel in Leinster Street, in central Dublin, having escaped her provincial native city and her difficult family in order to start a new life in the capital. She was not without character and, like many an attractive young girl, had had quite a number of admirers. When pressed by Joyce, she told him about the two most important and tragic cases – those of Michael Feeney, who had died aged just sixteen of typhoid, and of Michael Bodkin, who, on hearing she was to leave Galway, got out of his sickbed and walked through the streaming rain to her house to entreat her to stay. He died shortly afterwards of tuberculosis. Joyce would later have Gretta Conroy recount a similar story to her husband in the climactic scene of 'The Dead', and he would draw on every aspect of Nora's personality for the creation of all his important female characters, Bertha in *Exiles*, Molly Bloom in *Ulysses*, and Anna Livia Plurabelle in *Finnegans Wake*. Despite her lack of interest in Joyce's writing and her failure to read most of it, Nora was more than a match for Joyce and became his most vital inspiration after his father. The 'Penelope' episode of *Ulysses* is his lasting testament to her, his triumphantly lyrical celebration of his patient, simple, earthy, faithful Galway girl.

Initially Nora was a little puzzled when Joyce approached her and she took him for a foreign sailor. She failed to turn up for their first date, but on receiving a supplicatory letter from him, asking her to meet him on 16 June, she agreed without hesitation. They met, walked out to Ringsend and from that day on spent all her free time together. It was a fateful date, he told her, the day that she made a man of him. He later chose it for 'Bloomsday', the day on which the events of *Ulysses* take place.

In August he took her to a concert in which he was taking part along with John McCormack, the great Irish tenor, and others. It was to be the high point of Joyce's musical career. His mellifluous voice caught the attention of *The Freeman's Journal,* which recorded that Joyce, 'the possessor of a sweet tenor voice, sang charmingly "The Salley Gardens" and gave a pathetic rendering of "The Croppy Boy".' Nora was most impressed and, in later life, was often quoted as saying that he should have stuck to music instead of bothering with writing.

Joyce entered this relationship with unprecedented intensity and insisted that

The old Abbey Theatre, Dublin, which opened to the public in December 1904 with Yeats's On Baile's Strand *and* Cathleen ni Houlihan *and Lady Gregory's* Spreading the News *(Hulton Getty).*

Nora should know and accept everything about him. Despite their totally different backgrounds, interests and education, Joyce became convinced that she more than anyone else could understand him. On 15 September 1904, the night after he had fled Gogarty's tower, he came as close to proposing to Nora as he was able; they agreed to make their lives together and depart for Europe. Although he loved her deeply, he was not willing to accept the constraints of Catholic Irish society and marry her, thus exile provided the only way in which they could stay together according to his rules.

A street scene in Galway, Nora Barnacle's home town. The women are hiding their faces from a stranger's camera and, in some cases, taking flight (Hulton Getty).

2

'AND TRIESTE AH TRIESTE!'

When James and Nora arrived in the cosmopolitan Adriatic city of Trieste on 20 October 1904, they had been travelling together, on and off, for twelve days, having begun their odyssey on the ferry which had sailed on 8 October from Dublin's North Wall to Holyhead. He had been seen off by his father, his sister Poppie, his brother Stanislaus and his aunt Josephine, while Nora had boarded separately and alone, as her family knew nothing about her flight and Joyce had chosen to keep his father from knowing about her until after the event, much to his predictable consternation.

A romanticized poster of Trieste by Louis Cassas (Bridgeman Art Library / Victoria & Albert Museum).

Leaving Dublin, they passed through London and Paris before reaching Zurich, where they stayed for a week at the Gasthaus Hoffnung and consummated their *de facto* marriage. They were subsidized by Lady Gregory (five pounds), a disapproving George Russell (ten shillings), John Stanislaus Joyce and others. As Joyce put it when trying to convince acquaintances to help him pay for the trip: 'I am not like Jesus Christ, I can't walk on water.' He travelled in the belief that he had been accepted for a position at the Berlitz school in Zurich, but, when he arrived, the school director informed him politely that they had never heard of the agent who had promised him the job and that they had no vacancies. Joyce was left, therefore, with little choice but to follow the director's advice and undertake a further journey to a possible job in Trieste.

On their arrival in the Austro-Hungarian port of Trieste the couple were again met with the news that there was no vacancy at the local Berlitz school. All was not lost, however – a new school was opening in Pola and would require a second English teacher to complete its staff. Within a couple of days Almidano Artifoni, the owner of the school, arrived from Pola and formally hired Joyce (who later rewarded him by using his name for Stephen Dedalus's Italian teacher in *A Portrait of the Artist as a Young Man* and *Ulysses*). Now calling themselves Mr and Mrs Joyce, as Artifoni had suggested so as not to cause scandal or incur bureaucratic difficulties, the couple travelled down the beautiful Istrian coast and arrived in Pola on 30 October.

Their sojourn in the main Austro-Hungarian military port was short and unhappy. Although it was a reasonably cosmopolitan place with a mixed population of about fifty thousand Italians, Serbs, Croatians, Germans and Slovenes, they found it hard to settle down in their 'furnished room and kitchen, surrounded by pots, pans and kettles' in what Joyce described as 'a back-of-God-speed place – a naval Siberia'. Right from the start they lived beyond their means – a habit they would never break – and rarely dined at home, choosing instead to have food at a nearby trattoria before going on to the elegant Caffé Miramar, where they drank coffee and read the international newspapers before retreating reluctantly to their cold damp flat. In December they had to face the daunting realization that Nora was pregnant and were glad to be able to count on the support of Joyce's new Tuscan friend, Alessandro Francini Bruni,

Trieste's waterfront including (from left) Palazzo Carciotti, the Greek Orthodox Church of the Most Holy Trinity and San Nicolò, the Caffé Tommaseo and the Teatro Verdi. Joyce and Nora travelled down the Istrian coast from Trieste to Pola on the Graf Wurmbrand *in October 1904 (Archivio Fantin).*

who was also his immediate superior in the school. The two men got along well together, perhaps because of their similar educations and interests, and Joyce and Nora were delighted to accept Francini Bruni's invitation to share an apartment with him, his wife Clotilde and their little son Daniele.

The greater part of Joyce's day was spent at the Berlitz school, which was located near the Arch of Sergius in the city centre. He was an immediate success as a teacher, as well as an asset to the school with his Bachelor of Arts degree, and was reasonably pleased with his regular salary of '£2 a week for sixteen hours weekly'. Faced with a classroom of beginners who spoke a variety of languages and dialects, he had little choice but to follow faithfully Berlitz's *First Book*. Between lessons, he found time to complete more than a dozen chapters of *Stephen Hero* and to write several poems and more short stories for *Dubliners*, all of which he sent to Stanislaus for comment. Finally, having been unable to afford to do so in Dublin, he now had his 96-line broadside 'The Holy Office' printed and dispatched for distribution there. It was to be the last thing he would publish until March 1907.

As soon as the chance of a transfer to Trieste came, Joyce jumped at it and moved there in March 1905. Apart from three brief visits to Dublin, seven months in Rome, and the enforced escape to Zurich during the First World War, Trieste was to be his home for more than eleven years until 1920, as it had earlier been home to other distinguished visitors such as the French writer Stendhal, the Irish novelist Charles Lever and the celebrated English explorer and translator Sir Richard Burton, all of whom served as consuls there. Upon arrival, Joyce was impressed by the city's busy port, where ships from the Orient and several Italian ports queued to dock and unload their often exotic cargoes in a confusion of languages and dialects. It did not take the future writer of *Ulysses* — the epic of an eternal wanderer — long to understand the city's maritime vocation and its role as Austria's gateway to the Mediterranean, its only merchant seaport. Trieste had grown relentlessly in the nineteenth century, assuming a highly cosmopolitan middle-European flavour as a melting-pot of different cultures, even if the dominant Italian population was becoming increasingly resentful of Austro-Hungary's stubborn Germanization of the city and wary of the threat they saw coming from the Slav world.

Joyce began teaching at the Berlitz school and, although he found the daily grind wearing, he came to enjoy the company and friendship of quite a few of his lively array of students, but especially of two enormously wealthy Greek noblemen, Baron Ralli and Count Sordina. Another prominent pupil of his was Roberto Prezioso, the editor of the city's most important evening newspaper, *Il Piccolo della Sera*. Soon Joyce at least partially abandoned Berlitz's methods and transformed his lessons into informal conversations during which he laid down the law on a variety of subjects, from Italian and Irish literature to what he slightingly referred to as the great English contribution to modern civilization, the water closet. He also frequently referred to his own financial problems, which continued to be pressing and caused him to borrow money and to demand advances on his 45-crown weekly wage in his struggle to make ends meet and maintain 'a "gentlemanly" appearance . . . on a salary fit for a navvy'.

There was much in Trieste to hold his interest. He

liked visiting the many places of worship in this city which had thrived on religious tolerance and was home to Catholic, Jewish, Greek and Serb Orthodox communities, in addition to sizeable numbers of Armenian Mechitarists, Swiss and Valdesian Protestants, Lutherans, Anglicans and Methodists. 'Jimmy the chapelgoer', as Joyce calls himself in *Finnegans Wake*, especially liked going to the exotically ornate Greek Orthodox Church of the Most Holy Trinity and San Nicolò, the Serb Orthodox San Spiridione, the Jewish synagogue and various Catholic Churches which he favoured around Easter. Another of his entertainments was to go to the opera, especially to the *loggione* – the upper gallery – of the Teatro Comunale 'Giuseppe Verdi', or to the imposing Teatro Politeama Rossetti, both of which mounted impressive seasons. Mahler, Toscanini and Mascagni were just three of the famous *maestri* who came to conduct in Joyce's time, and in the Triestines they would have found one of the best prepared and most critical audiences in Europe. In *Giacomo Joyce*, his later Triestine novelette, Joyce left a memorable impression in the style of D'Annunzio

Trieste was a cosmopolitan centre of fashion and Corso Italia was its main shopping street. For a brief period in 1907 the Joyces lived in an apartment which looked out over the Corso and Joyce had ample chance to note that 'the Trieste people are great "stylists" in dress, often starving themselves in order to be able to flaunt good dresses' (Archivio Fantin).

The Church of Sant' Antonio Taumaturgo or St Anthony the Worker of Miracles. When writing Finnegans Wake, *Joyce liked to link the River Liffey in Dublin with the Canal Grande in Trieste through the person of Italo Svevo's wife, Livia. He thus wrote to Svevo on 21 November 1925: 'Reassure your wife with regard to the character Anna Livia. I have taken only her hair, and that merely as a loan, to adorn the little river of my city, the Anna Liffey, which would be the longest river in the world if it were not for the canal which comes from afar to join the celebrated divo, Anthony the Worker of Miracles, and then, having changed its mind, returns whence it came' (Archivio Fantin).*

of the *loggione* in the Teatro Verdi:

> Loggione. The sodden walls ooze a steamy damp. A symphony of smells fuses the mass of huddled human forms: sour reek of armpits, nozzled oranges, melting breast ointments, mastick water, the breath of suppers of sulphurous garlic, phosphorescent farts, opoponax, the frank sweat of marriageable and married womankind, the soapy stink of men...

He was also fascinated by the astonishing mixture of languages to be heard in the city's streets and by the *Triestino* dialect, the linguistic glue which bound together so many peoples 'from all the ends of Europe'. *Triestino* was an inclusive force which embraced different civilizations and became a living encyclopaedia of the cultures, nations and languages which had been assimilated within the city. Later, when writing his own encyclopaedia of world culture in *Finnegans Wake*, Joyce would create an international portmanteau language, rooted in English but brimming with different traditions, in which few individual words could be safely reduced to one single, authoritative meaning. And in this respect the language of *Finnegans Wake* is like an exaggerated, exploded version of *Triestino*, that rich, composite dialect which Joyce listened to with rapt attention and learned to speak brilliantly.

As the exceptionally hot summer of 1905 progressed, Nora was nearing the end of her term and became so depressed that Joyce wrote telling Stanislaus that she was always crying and quite helpless. It is difficult not to pity her, all day alone in a stuffy apartment, heavily pregnant and worrying about how much James was drinking and how they would provide for the child when it was born. She depended on him entirely, and yet she did not have the security that only marriage could bring.

Unexpected support came from their landlady, Signora Moise Canarutto, who had a soft spot for this strange young foreign couple she had taken in, and who was glad to assist at Giorgio's birth on 29 July 1905. Joyce was delighted with the new arrival and found Giorgio 'fat and very quiet', and rather amusing. But with his birth came fresh worries. Joyce was all too aware that their already precarious financial situation would become more acute, although with Stanislaus he tried to deny this new reality and declared paternity 'a legal fiction'. The presence of a baby in the house made it more difficult for him to write and his frustration at this new situation is reflected in the short story in *Dubliners* entitled 'A Little Cloud'. In this story the hero, Little Chandler, a petty clerk with thwarted literary aspirations, feels rage and frustration surge within him when his attempts to read Byron are interrupted by the crying of his child. It is also significant that Little Chandler finds himself attracted by the idea of 'rich Jewesses. Those dark Oriental eyes, he thought, how full they are of passion, of voluptuous longing!'

Joyce, too, appears to have been attracted by the 'dark Oriental eyes' of at least one of his fascinating young female students: Annie Schleimer. Annie was a typical *Triestina*, an elegant half-Italian girl of Jewish extraction, the speaker of several languages, an accomplished pianist, and the first of several such women who would enthral and inspire Joyce over the coming decades. Such a lady is the object of desire in

Stanislaus Joyce (1884 – 1955) was the first person to recognise his brother's genius and played a vital role in Dublin and Trieste in encouraging him to keep at his writing despite the material problems around him. Stanislaus moved to Trieste in 1905 and worked tirelessly there to keep James and his family, and was rarely thanked for his trouble. As Joyce put it in Ulysses: *'A brother is as easily forgotten as an umbrella.' Stanislaus died on Bloomsday, 16 June 1955 (Cornell University Library).*

Giacomo Joyce, Joyce's important transitional work in poetic prose, which he wrote between 1911 and 1914. It chronicles a down-at-heel English teacher's attraction towards his sophisticated student and reveals Joyce's earliest experiments with the interior monologue which he would later develop in *Ulysses*.

Back in 1905 Joyce was so overwhelmed by his problems with Nora and the demands of fatherhood that he sought help from the ever reliable Stanislaus by

NOVELS

THE LIGHT SIDE OF LITERATURE.

THE earnest people who take kindly to instruction have their share of the novels this month, although the frivolous who insist on sheer joy are not forgotten. Looking back on this contentious summer, future students will do well to consider the interpretations of the current book-shelf. Realism, satire, romance, fantasy—all damp from the press, and packed as close as peas! We cannot pretend to be still the stodgy British, suspecting carnal indulgence in anything original. The young authors are not afraid to think aloud—biliously, or optimistically, or socialistically, according to their several conditions. They have learned their good French lesson, and they have become nothing if not versatile.

Mr. H. H. Munro's "BEASTS AND SUPER-BEASTS" (*The Bodley Head*) is the *hors d'œuvre* before more solid meats. "Saki," as we all know, abhors the serious purpose, though no one can better give it a passing fillip. Once, and brilliantly, he preached on the dangers of decadence, and we fancy the new collection of stories may have been thrown off in a fine reaction from "When William Came." It is not without its decadents, but they are subordinated to an irresponsible spirit. Clovis is certainly not a moralist, and Clovis reappears in many of these stories. There is also

MR. LAURENCE HOUSMAN,
Who has just published another "Jingaloo" tale, "A Royal Runaway."—*[Photograph by Bassano.]*

a young person, sex female, age about fifteen, who is an artist in the manufacture of practical jokes at the expense of grown-up people. She belongs to "the classes"; but in other respects she is kin to Mr. Barry Pain's schoolgirl, whose genius for reducing shop-assistants to frenzy was the abiding glory of "Nothing Serious." Is she a type? A product of education on the lines laid down by Mr. Bernard Shaw? Romance at short notice was her specialty, and she applied it to making adults uncomfortable. But there are other people in the book who enjoy doing unexpected things. Lady Carlotta, left behind at a wayside station, was accosted by an unsuspecting matron in this form of words: "You must be Miss Hope, the governess I've come to meet." "Very well; if I must, I must," Lady Carlotta said to herself with dangerous meekness—and proceeded to hold revel in the bosom of the Quabarl family, where her practice of the Schartz-Metterklume system of instruction (invented on the spur of the moment) produced nerve-shattering effects upon Mrs. Quabarl. Another inspiration must be noticed before we leave Mr. Munro. He has invented the most exasperating jingle since "Punch, brothers, punch." Lucas Harrowcluff conceived a music-hall melody with the refrain—

> Cousin Teresa takes out Cæsar,
> Fido, Jack, and the big borzoi.

Big-drum business on the two syllables of bor-zoi. It is fatally easy to see why it took London by storm. "Cousin Teresa takes out Cæsar"—the thing has an abominable fascination, with or without the big drum *obbligato*.

Larry's most damaging charge against the Irish in "John Bull's Other Island" was that they were a mean-spirited nation. He rent asunder the veil from their dreaming, and pointed out that it was a

MR. JAMES JOYCE,
The author of a remarkably clever book of short stories entitled "Dubliners."

pernicious, drugging thing, far removed from the lofty vision of the idealist. "DUBLINERS" (*Grant Richards*) could give him powder and shot: Mr. James Joyce's studies are not, strictly speaking, fiction. They are facts shifted and sorted in the kaleidoscope of a novelist's brain—not at all the same thing. The impression they leave is sordid, unilluminated, circumscribed. It draws a sharp picture of narrow and ignoble lives. The sentimental Irishman of the English fancy is, of course, absent: by this time he should be dead as the dodo. Mr. Joyce's Dubliners are drab, rather dirty-minded, rather suspicious, and superstitious materialists. They are, in fact, a people who have lost the self-respect of freemen—a people, to put it clearly, ripe for Tammany. They furnish a very strong reason for the Celtic revival, for if they are as they are drawn here their case is desperate, and only the prophet or the seer can hope to mend them. Handled by politicians for their own ends, they do not bear thinking about. The bright spot in the book is "Maria"—and a nation is not saved by the virtues of its aged virgins. We should prefer **not** to believe in Mr. Joyce's dreary realism; **but**, unfortunately, he has the touch of genius. "Dubliners," whether you like it or not, is a book to be reckoned with.

The kingdom of Jingalo is a locality, elusive of exact identification, where the foibles of a

THE INHABITANTS OF "THE VALLEY OF THE MOON":
MR. AND MRS. JACK LONDON.

Mr. Jack London's "John Barleycorn" is reviewed on this page.
Photograph the Copyright of Mills and Boon, Ltd., London.

democratic constitution can be followed through Mr. Laurence Housman's glasses. King John of Jingalo proceeds with his career in "THE ROYAL RUNAWAY" (*Chapman and Hall*). A limited monarchy, Mr. Housman points out, has an unlimited capacity for futilities. John of Jingalo, poor dear, bereft of his practical Queen, and wearied of the meshes of the constitution, escaped to a small cathedral town, where a respectable landlady took him on his face value as an insignificant elderly gentleman, and gave him balm, tea and toast, and slippers by the fire. "The Royal Runaway" is a clever satire. Its sarcasms have sometimes a deodorising, broad whiff of humour—witness the legend of the foundation of the august Order of the Suspender. If the Garter, why not the Suspender? We laugh, but with a wry mouth, touched in our windy dignity. There is a deadly thrust in the account of the destruction of King Fritz's Central South American kingdom, where he held missionaries and traders at bay, to the great peace and comfort of his people, until the manner of their expulsion wounded the self-esteem of the United States. "Americans have many good qualities, but they are the vainest creatures on God's earth.... Outraged individualism grew rampant in sixty million breasts of Star-and-Stripishness. And,

following that, a flight of aeroplanes came and dropped bombs on the King and Queen and their urchin Princelings, the hope of the new rising race. At the death of their King, the Attapecs scattered back into nature-loving savagery, and English, Americans, and Europeans came in and commercialised the country.... And between whiles, for a diversion, they violated the women, and, taking some into enforced concubinage, got their civilised throats cut during sleep as a consequence. This, of course, led to practical extermination, for 'sex-war' thus treacherously conducted was not to be endured." And so "The Royal Runaway" grimaces, like a dreadful little hunchback in cap and bells, mocking his own and our infirmity.

There is escape from satire and realism alike in "THE STORY OF FIFINE" (*Constable*). It is frankly an idyll. Mr. Bernard Capes is a modern who likes to take leaves out of the books of the old romancers. Fifine and Felix wander together from Paris to Provence, and fair is the story of their love, and fortunate are they that the sympathetic Mr. Capes has set it down unsmirched. Boccaccio would have made a comedy of it whereat all his ladies would have blushed and laughed. Mr. Capes, being a modern, better suits the modern taste. It has a charming atmosphere, and here is the text: "The unexpected is the salt of life ..., one would rather chance encountering the unexpected in excess than be without it altogether." Surely a very proper sentiment for the complete romantic writer.

MR. BERNARD CAPES,
The well-known novelist, whose latest book is reviewed on this page.—*[Photo. by Elliott and Fry.]*

These "alcoholic memoirs" of Mr. Jack London are alive with the vigour of their author. No man before has written an autobiography quite like this, and it is well that it should be done—once. "JOHN BARLEYCORN" (*Mills and Boon*) is the story of Jack London, with the alcoholic interest put first and the rest subordinated to it. His encounters with the drink, his armed truce with the drink, his reflections upon the drink are thrust into the foremost place, and, frankly, we fear that more than justice is done to them. Mr. London remarks that he is not a "chemical alcoholic"—a man in whom alcohol satisfies a physical need—and he then exposes the convivial temptations, and the solacing temptations, and the drugging temptations of "Come and have a drink." He begins with himself as a too-enterprising youngster, dipping into the dinner pail of beer. He ends with a plea for the abolition of alcohol

MR. H. H. MUNRO,
The writer of short stories under the pseudonym of "Saki," whose book, "Beasts and Super-Beasts," has just been published.—*[Photograph by Hoppé.]*

from the lives of the coming generations. Has he, we wonder, read Archdall Reid, and reflected how his own immunity—according to that scientific observer—has come about? The story he tells is an eloquent testimony to the splendid stamina of the true American stock to which it is his proud boast that he belongs. It is the history of a great adventurer; and its alcoholic side does nothing to devitalise it. Great indeed is the fibre of the man who has "made good" after these hazards. But will adventure-loving youth, reading "John Barleycorn," perceive an awful example, and cleave to abstinence? We doubt it.

---

inviting him to come and join them. In October 1905 Stannie arrived from Dublin and was shocked by the poor state of relations between Joyce and Nora, by Joyce's restlessness, Nora's bad temper and the bitter atmosphere in their apartment. He did his best to put things right and from the moment of his arrival, apart from resuming his role as the whetstone on which Jim sharpened his ideas, he shouldered almost single-handedly the burden of maintaining an uneasy domestic peace and of keeping

A page from the Literary Supplement to the Illustrated London News of 1 August 1914 with a glowing review of Dubliners. Joyce is in *eminent company here (Bridgeman Art Library / Illustrated London News Picture Library).*

the household afloat by paying for most of the essentials – rent, food and clothes for the whole family – from the modest salary he earned as a teacher of English in his new position at the Berlitz school. Joyce, meanwhile, continued to spend flamboyantly on his own priorities – books, theatre, drink and dining out.

By early 1906 *Dubliners*, consisting of twelve stories, was finished and had been dispatched to Grant Richards in London. Joyce was generally pleased with the stories and hoped he would soon be able to afford his fellow Irishmen the opportunity of seeing themselves in his 'nicely polished looking-glass'. But publication was to prove far more difficult than he could ever have imagined. He became locked into inconclusive negotiations with Richards, who demanded that he make a series of changes to 'Counterparts' and particularly to a new story he had added entitled 'Two Gallants'. Thus began a battle which cost Joyce dearly and which would take until 1915 to resolve.

So deeply discouraged was Joyce that he decided a fresh start was needed; as a result he began to think seriously about leaving Trieste. In early May he applied and was accepted for a job in the Nast-Kolb & Schumacher Bank in Rome, believing that he would earn almost double the money in the bank for fewer hours of work and would, therefore, be able to devote more time to his writing. It was a serious miscalculation.

Joyce, Nora and Giorgio arrived in Rome on 31 July 1906 full of optimism, but little or nothing went right for them in the Eternal City, which they fled after just seven months, in March 1907. Joyce laboured under a demanding and dull workload in the bank, he encountered problems securing affordable and decent accommodation and he soon realized that he did not care for the Romans, who he compared to 'a man who lives by exhibiting to travellers his grandmother's corpse'. In whatever little time was left him after work he distracted and amused himself by reading the anti-clerical writings in the satirical paper *L'Asino* and by following the pronouncements of the socialists Enrico Ferri and Arturo Labriola in the socialist paper *L'Avanti*. He also took a considerable interest in matters religious, but seeing the pomp and opulence of the Catholic Church at such close quarters only served to alienate him further from it.

In late November he took a second job in the *École de Langues*, which meant that after working until seven in the bank he taught nightly for three hours until 10.15, but still they struggled to make ends meet. Christmas – 'we shall dine on paste', he wrote to Stanislaus – brought no cheer either, rather it evoked nostalgia for Dublin and probably contributed to the sumptuousness of the Christmas dinner Joyce described in such lavish detail in 'The Dead'.

Indeed, it was in Rome that Joyce began writing this story, which is by far the longest in *Dubliners* and is something of a corrective to the bleak vision of Dublin presented in the rest of the book, a vision which Joyce began to feel was 'unnecessarily harsh'. More ambitious than the other stories in its thematic and stylistic scope, 'The Dead' masterfully blends the private and public themes of the earlier stories, and transcends all of them in its stylistic and linguistic perfection. An astonishingly mature achievement for a man just twenty-five years of age, it develops themes explored earlier, such as marriage, the relationships between the sexes, the generations and the social classes, and furnishes a detailed exploration not only of Gabriel and

Gretta and their marriage, but also of Ireland, its history, culture and politics.

Meanwhile life with Nora and Giorgio continued as before even if poor Nora was even more a fish out of water in Rome than she had been in Trieste. Soon their situation was to become even more difficult when they discovered that she was again pregnant. This news brought further pressure to bear on both of them, but especially on Joyce, who now talked of his flight to Rome as a 'folly', describing the city as 'the stupidest old whore of a town' he was ever in. Soon he began to feel drawn back to Trieste, remembering 'some nights walking along the streets in the summer and thinking over some of the phrases in my stories'. On St Valentine's Day 1907 he sent a telegram to his brother requesting him to send money to allow him to come back: 'Given notice returning Trieste send forty urgent monte brianza [sic] wire if Artifoni accepts'. Although Stanislaus discouraged him, a most unfortunate event brought his purgatory to an end on 6 March. Having just received his monthly salary, Joyce was robbed and arrested in a subsequent brawl. By the time he struggled back home to Nora, his mind was made up. He wired Stanislaus and with Nora and Giorgio, began the journey home to Trieste.

The Caffé Bizantino was one of Trieste's many oriental coffee houses. The Joyces lived in the second house on the right, on the third floor, above the Farmacia Picciola at No 32 via della Barriera Vecchia from August 1910 to September 1912 (Archivio Fantin).

Back in the Adriatic port Joyce was once again penniless and jobless and, when Stanislaus pointed this out, his response was, 'Well, then, I have you.' Luckily for Joyce, several of his acquaintances were also willing to help him get back on his feet. Francini Bruni took the Joyces into his flat for a time, and Artifoni agreed to rehire him at 15 crowns for six hours' teaching per week at the Berlitz school. In May 1907 *Chamber Music* was published, but perhaps an even more significant event was Joyce's becoming English tutor to the half-Italian and half-German Jewish Triestine writer Ettore Schmitz, who was better known by his pen-name Italo Svevo. A frustrated novelist who made a good living running the ships' varnish factory owned by his wife's family, Schmitz was impressed by Joyce and his bohemian way of life, and within a short time was talking literature with him during lessons. Joyce brought Svevo *Chamber Music* and the stories of *Dubliners* to read, and in turn read Svevo's accomplished, but critically unacclaimed, early novels. The Triestine writer was so overjoyed with his young teacher's reaction to his *Senilità* that he began to write once again after a long period of silence, and many years later credited Joyce with having worked the miracle of Lazarus on him. The favour was returned in 1909, almost a year after Joyce had abandoned his new version of *A Portrait of the Artist as a Young Man* after three chapters. It took all of Svevo's enthusiasm for this abandoned work to rouse the struggling Irish writer back into reworking the final chapters. Svevo would soon have an even bigger role to play in Joyce's literary universe and would serve as an initially unwitting prototype for Leopold Bloom, the protagonist of *Ulysses*. Joyce bombarded

Joyce enjoyed a genuine literary friendship with Italo Svevo (1861–1928). In 1927 the latter wrote of Joyce: 'He is twice a rebel against England and against Ireland. He hates England and would like to transform Ireland. Yet he belongs so much to England that like a great many of his Irish predecessors he will fill pages of English literary history and not the least splendid ones; and he is so Irish that the English have no love for him, and there is no doubt that his success could never have been achieved in England if France and some literary Americans had not imposed it' (Archivio Svevo, Biblioteca Civica, Trieste).

him with so many questions about the Jews that one day, during a lesson with Stanislaus, Svevo said: 'Tell me some secrets about Irishmen. You know your brother has been asking me so many questions about Jews that I want to get even with him.'

Shortly after his return from Rome, Joyce's former student Roberto Prezioso asked him to write some articles about Ireland for *Il Piccolo della Sera*, which, together with *Il Piccolo*, was Trieste's leading organ of irredentism (the movement to return all Italian-speaking regions in the Austro-Hungarian empire to Italy). Meanwhile Attilio Tamaro, a prominent irredentist propagandist and writer, invited him to lecture at the *Università Popolare*. Both hoped to make propaganda out of Joyce's contributions about Ireland's situation within the British Empire, which paralleled that of Trieste within Austro-Hungary. These invitations drew Joyce away from his interest in socialism, which had peaked and waned in Rome, and provided him with an opportunity to study the nationalist politics of Trieste. Although Joyce had a couple

Joyce wrote nine articles for Trieste's leading evening paper, Il Piccolo della Sera, *which was edited by his friend and student Roberto Prezioso and owned by Teodoro Mayer, long considered a model for Leopold Bloom because of his Hungarian Jewish descent (Archivio Fantin).*

of irredentist friends, such as the writer Silvio Benco (a Triestine version of D'Annunzio) and the multilingual lawyer Nicolò Vidacovich (a highly skilled translator and noted essayist), he never committed himself to their creed. Even if he did make a minor contribution to their cause, he always remained as dubious about irredentism, in what he called 'old Auster and Hungrig' in *Finnegans Wake*, as he was about nationalism in Ireland or anywhere else. In Herbert Gorman's biography of him Joyce saw to it that the description of his sojourn in the Austro-Hungarian empire was fond and appreciative:

> I cannot begin to give you the flavour of the old Austrian Empire. It was a ramshackle affair but it was charming, gay, and I experienced more kindnesses in Trieste than ever before or since in my life... Times past cannot return but I wish they were back.

In total he wrote nine front-page leading articles, in perfect Italian, in the space often filled by leading Italian thinkers such as Arturo Labriola and Guglielmo Ferrero, for *Il Piccolo della Sera*, which enjoyed a readership at least equal to that of Dublin's *Freeman's Journal*. He chose what he referred to as 'the turbid drama of Fenianism' as the topic for his first article on 22 March 1907, using John O'Leary's

On 27 April 1907 Joyce gave his lecture in Italian entitled 'Ireland: Island of Saints and Sages' to an audience of some one hundred Triestines in the sala della Borsa, the columned building featured in this photograph. For the occasion he had to borrow a suit belonging to Almidano Artifoni, the director of the Berlitz School (Archivio Fantin).

death as the focus for his comments. His second, 'Home Rule Comes of Age', was a more substantial piece, surveying a century of Anglo-Irish relations and the awful disappointments offered by history. It showed that no matter how great Joyce's fascination with the Irish situation, he neither had faith in nor wished to serve the Irish cause directly. The third article, 'Ireland at the Bar', was his strongest statement yet on what he termed the 'snarled' Irish question. Joyce's overall intention was rather closely aligned to that of Sinn Fein; he wished to make Ireland's case in Europe and to counter the anti-Irish reports that made their way into the Italian papers through English news agencies.

In the 'Ireland, Island of Saints and Sages' lecture which he read in a borrowed suit before an audience of some one hundred Triestines at the Università Popolare, Joyce provided a rich survey of Ireland, its history and culture. He focused on the role played by early Irish Catholicism in forming the Irish and, by extension, the European mind, and described the ancient times 'when the island was a true focus of sanctity and intellect, spreading throughout the continent a culture and a vitalizing energy'. He emphasized that over these centuries Ireland's links were not with Britain, but with Europe, and he lauded Irishmen like Columbanus for carrying their learning abroad. All of this had a personal relevance for Joyce, who was seeking Irish precedents for his own very European literary enterprise.

This period of Joyce's life was punctuated by bouts of heavy drinking in a variety of Trieste's 600-odd bars. Although he never imbibed during the day, the evenings were a different matter and he was never short of companions to join him. He enjoyed speaking with the locals in their dialect and often joined them in singing as the night developed. But his capacity for alcohol was limited and, since he got drunk quickly, sometimes Francini Bruni or Stanislaus had to go out to find him and carry him home. His nightly shenanigans annoyed Nora and enraged Stanislaus, who not only had to support his brother's family but also often had to attempt to negotiate peace between the couple. In the summer of 1907, after a night out drinking with some Triestine companions, Joyce ended up in a gutter and subsequently suffered a severe attack of rheumatic fever, which caused him to be confined to bed for several weeks and was one of the causes of the deterioration in his eyesight which was to become acute in Zurich. This illness led to a row with Artifoni over sick-pay and Joyce used this as an excuse to resign his Berlitz school post.

Joyce was a regular visitor to the Teatro Politeama Rossetti, Trieste, which offered generous seasons of opera and prose. On 12 January 1910 a famous futurist evening was held there, featuring Filippo Tommaso Marinetti, Aldo Palazzeschi and Armando Mazza. This event confirmed Trieste's status as one of the three capitals of futurism together with Paris and Milan (Archivio Fantin).

Luckily, by 25 July, he was well enough to take Nora to the *Ospedale Maggiore*, where she gave birth the next morning to their second child, Lucia. Both parents were slightly disappointed, as they had been hoping for another boy, but they soon recovered and were glad of the twenty crowns given them in charity when Nora was discharged from the hospital's poor ward on 5 August.

As the autumn progressed Joyce began to pick up private lessons, but now his income was more paltry than ever. Had it not been for Stanislaus, who had stayed on at the Berlitz, they might have ended on the street. Joyce justified his lack of work and turned it to his advantage by focusing on his writing, and by the end of September 1907 had finished 'The Dead' and begun rewriting *Stephen Hero* as *A Portrait of the Artist as a Young Man*.

Relations within the Joyce household were only intermittently serene and the three adults there – Jim, Nora and Stannie – all strong-minded and stubborn, struggled to get along together. Joyce's relationship with Nora fluctuated between moments of great tenseness, of genuine fondness, of lively sexual encounters (she had a miscarriage in August 1908 to her relief and his regret), of silence, bad temper and sulks. Clearly the greater burden of looking after the two young children fell upon her, and it weighed heavily since neither Giorgio nor Lucia was an easy child. Stanislaus's presence also seems to have created almost as many problems as it solved. He deeply resented Joyce's drinking and his treatment of Nora, of whom he

Teatro Verdi, Trieste. Here, in Joyce's time, a wide selection of European operas were performed and leading conductors, such as Toscanini, Mahler and Mascagni, took the podium (Museo Schmidl, Trieste).

himself had grown fond, and he was angry at how she would inevitably accept her companion's apologies for whatever excesses he was guilty of. He was also hurt by the knowledge that, despite her initial protests, Nora would inevitably side with Jim against him. He complained about the extravagant gifts Joyce gave her and about being taken for granted by both of them, and he resented being pressurized into constantly asking for advances on his salary in order to keep his brother's family afloat. Despite their increasingly frequent differences, the two brothers did sometimes get along well, enjoyed each another's company and often went out for long walks around the city, along the sea and into the Carso hills, or visited the theatre, where there was also something deserving of their attention. But these moments became rarer as the years passed.

Joyce was the more prolific theatre-goer and often managed to inveigle a free ticket out of his friends at *Il Piccolo*, although he mostly paid his own way into the cheaper seats, caring little what other sacrifices the family had to make in order for him to do so. He attended *Hamlet* at the Teatro Fenice, saw La Duse in

Rosmersholm at the Verdi, was enchanted by Puccini's *La Bohème* (which he saw eight times in two weeks) and enjoyed Catalani's *La Wally*. He was rather more perplexed by Wagner's *I Maestri Cantori di Norimberga*, although sometime between May and July 1909 he did sing in the quintet from the same opera, probably in a concert organized by his new singing teacher, Romeo Bartoli, the choirmaster for the Teatro Verdi and director of the city's highly regarded madrigal choir.

In March 1909 Joyce published his article 'Oscar Wilde: Il Poeta di "Salomè"' in *Il Piccolo della Sera* to coincide with the Trieste premiere of Strauss's *Salomè*. His writing was rather fitful at this time, even though the spring saw him returning to work on *A Portrait of the Artist as a Young Man* and translating Synge's *Riders to the Sea* with his friend Nicolò Vidacovich, with whom he would also translate Yeats's *The Countess Cathleen*.

In 1908 Joyce seriously considered becoming a professional tenor and enrolled for singing lessons at the Conservatory of Music in Trieste with Romeo Bartoli (1875–1936) as his teacher. The lessons ceased after two years, probably because Joyce ran out of money (Museo Schmidl, Trieste).

Gemma Bellincioni was a leading Italian soprano and a regular performer in Trieste. In 1909 she caught Joyce's attention when she sang the title role in Strauss's Salomé. *He used this production as an opportunity to write an article entitled 'Oscar Wilde: il poeta di "Salomé"' for* Il Piccolo della Sera *(Museo Schmidl, Trieste).*

Joyce went to Dublin in July and August 1909 to mend relations with his father, to take Giorgio to meet his grandparents, and to secure a contract for the publication of *Dubliners* with Maunsel & Co. The first aim he achieved without much difficulty. Too similar to get on together for a protracted period of time, father and son still understood each other well, and, when the former sat down at a piano in a bar and played the 'Di Provenza il mar' aria from *La Traviata,* in which Alfredo's father seeks reconciliation with his son by recalling his childhood in Provence, Joyce understood that he had been forgiven for his flight from Ireland with Nora. He also appeared to be making progress towards the publication of *Dubliners* when he agreed to a draft contract with Maunsel & Co., stating that his book would be in print by March 1910.

However, all of these positive developments were overshadowed by a meeting with his old college companion, Vincent Cosgrave, who informed him that he had walked out with Nora around the time she fell for Joyce. He was devastated by this news and immediately wrote a series of accusatory letters to Nora, going so far as to ask her: 'Is Georgie my son?' He wanted to return immediately to Trieste, and would have done so if Stanislaus had agreed to send him his fare and had he not met his old friend Byrne, who convinced him that the story was a plot hatched by Cosgrave and Gogarty to ruin him. Stanislaus also weighed in with evidence from Trieste that Nora had rebuffed Cosgrave in 1904, and eventually their combined efforts succeeded in calming Joyce. Soon he was begging her forgiveness. Years later Joyce would draw on this episode to make betrayal one of the central issues in *Ulysses*, where

Joyce spent a short period in an apartment overlooking the Piazza Ponterosso and the Canal Grande, which was filled with sailing ships unloading their cargoes (Archivio Fantin).

Cosgrave appears as Lynch, a Judas character who in 'Circe' abandons Stephen to the British soldiers and goes off with the prostitute Kitty Ricketts.

Joyce then travelled to the west of Ireland for a successful encounter with Nora's family, but in reality he wanted to get back to her in Trieste and soon began to prepare for the journey home. He arranged to take his sister Eva with him in the hope she would be company and help for Nora, and because he had been shocked at the conditions in which his many sisters were living in Dublin. In his letters he wrote of his longing to see Nora in *'la nostra bella Trieste'*, his desire to see the 'lights twinkling along the *riva* as the train passes Miramar', and it was clear that by now Trieste and Nora had somehow merged in his mind. It was the city which had sheltered him, she was the woman who had stood by him, and together they represented home.

Although Eva would never really settle in Trieste, she did soon mention that there was one aspect of the city which appealed to her – its cinemas – and went on to remark on how strange it was that Dublin had none. Joyce decided this was his chance to solve his financial problems, reckoning that, if Trieste could support twenty-one cinemas, surely Dublin could support one. He took his idea to Nicolò Vidacovich and together they found three business partners – Antonio Machnich, Giuseppe Caris and Giovanni Rebez – all of whom owned and ran cinemas in the city. The contract signed on 16 October was favourable to Joyce: the others would invest all the capital while he would receive ten per cent of any profits and would not be liable for any losses. Financed by his partners, the pioneer of Irish cinema set off again for Dublin in mid-October 1909, just weeks after his return to Trieste.

None of his family was happy to see him leave. Stanislaus doubted that the project would be successful and resented being left once more to shoulder the financial burden of the Trieste branch of the family, while Nora, for her part, was upset at being abandoned again after such a short time. But Joyce was not to be stopped. Within a week he had found suitable premises for the cinema in Mary Street. Throughout November and December he busied himself with preparations until finally the cinema opened, just before Christmas, with Pathé's *The Bewitched Castle* and *The First Paris Orphanage*, Caserini's or Pathé's *Beatrice Cenci*, an Italian production called *Devilled Crab*, and *La Pouponnière*. The next day the *Evening Telegraph* commented that although 'the tragic story of *Beatrice Cenci* was hardly as exhilarating a subject as one would desire on the eve of the festive season... the occasion may be described as

having been particularly successful.' At the end of December Joyce succeeded in getting a permanent licence for the cinema and soon set off again for Trieste (this time with another sister, Eileen, in tow), leaving a non-English-speaking Triestine manager called Novak in charge. It was a fatal error: soon the audiences began to fall and just six months later the cinema was sold at a loss of over £600.

While he was in Dublin, Nora became increasingly enraged with Joyce and in mid-November she threatened to leave him, because their landlord had demanded his rent, which neither she nor Stanislaus had the means to pay. Joyce sent instructions as to how to handle the landlord, bombarded her with letters, some supplicatory, others sexually explicit, and a new process of reconciliation and bonding began. Soon homecoming was in sight, and she was not only to prepare herself for him in her role as domineering lover, but also as a mother figure. 'Try', he wrote, 'to shelter me, dearest, from the storms of the world... . when I reach Via Scussa I will just creep into bed, kiss you tenderly on the forehead, curl myself up in the blankets and sleep, sleep, sleep. Darling, I am so glad you like my picture as a child... Oh *how supremely happy I shall be! ... I figlioli, il fuoco, una buona mangiata, un caffè nero, un Brasil, il Piccolo della Sera, e* Nora, Nora *mia*, Norina, Noretta, Norella, Noruccia...'

Back in Trieste, Joyce received good news in the autumn of 1910, when he was appointed to teach English at the evening school of the *Società degli Impiegati Civili*, a training school for clerks. He was obliged to teach for a mere three hours per week and the salary was low, so he continued to give private lessons. Later, in July 1913, he was appointed to a further teaching position at the prestigious economics institute, the *Scuola Superiore di Commercio* 'Revoltella', where he taught six hours per week and was paid 1,500 crowns per month – a not inconsiderable sum although 500 crowns less than the porter earned. *Il professore Joyce*, or 'Zois', as his Triestine students called him, also supplemented his income by dabbling in the woollen retail business. A series of letters and invoices to and from the Dublin Woollen Company in 1910 and 1911 reveal that the usually impecunious writer was taking to heart the Woollen Company's motto 'An ounce of practice is worth a ton of theory' and making quite a success of selling suits, homespuns and tweeds to a long list of his Triestine acquaintances.

While these activities undoubtedly helped keep hunger at bay, his literary ambitions still languished as he had not yet managed to get *Dubliners* into print. By the summer of 1911 Maunsel & Co. were still procrastinating and demanding so many cuts and changes that the exasperated writer sent them a dramatic ultimatum and eventually took the extraordinary step of making his situation public by sending letters to Arthur Griffith's newspaper *Sinn Féin* and to the *Northern Whig* of Belfast. Unfortunately Maunsel & Co. were unmoved and, even though Joyce did muster sympathy for his predicament, his book remained unpublished and unknown.

In the summer of 1912 he decided it was time that Nora, who had not been home since leaving Ireland in 1904, had a trip there. She was delighted to escape what he called 'that damn silly sun that turns men into butter' and soon departed with Lucia, leaving Jim alone with Giorgio in Trieste. Upon arrival in Dublin she went to press her husband's case with Maunsel & Co.

before going down to Galway. Meanwhile, in Trieste, Joyce became deeply worried when he failed to receive a letter from her announcing her safe arrival in Ireland and was disappointed when he received just a scribbled postcard five days after her departure. He dashed off an angry and melodramatic reply, demanding to know how she could care so little about him after all they had been through together and informing her that he was departing immediately for Ireland with Giorgio.

As soon as he reached Dublin he began a new spiral of inconclusive negotiations with George Roberts of Maunsel & Co. before travelling on to Galway to see Nora, who was pleased that her absence had inspired such a passionate display of anger. He toured Galway with her and found time to write two articles for *Il Piccolo della Sera*. He also cycled to Oughterard and went on a trip to the Aran Islands before returning to Dublin, where he made a valiant but futile attempt to reach agreement with Roberts before deciding that the only way forward was to publish the collection himself. Thus he agreed to buy 100-odd copies from Maunsel & Co. for £15, which he intended to have brought out by Falconer, Maunsel's printer, under the imprint of the 'Liffey Press'. Unfortunately, Falconer's Catholic sensibilities were offended by the content of the stories and he refused to hand over the sheets, announcing that he was going to destroy them. Although Joyce managed to obtain at least one complete set before this threat was carried out, this was not only the end of *Dubliners* as far as Dublin was concerned but also the end of Dublin as far as Joyce was concerned. He left that very night for London and, during his return journey, he exorcised the ghosts of Roberts and Falconer by writing his satirical poem 'Gas

from a Burner' in a tone of unswerving bitterness. He would never again return to Ireland, because now he knew what he had long suspected: home was no longer there, and exile was no longer a choice, but an obligation.

In Joyce's absence there had been more landlord problems in Trieste. However, Stanislaus, who by now lived in separate accommodation, managed to find them a fine new second-floor flat on via Bramante, overlooking Piazza Vico, which would be their home until the outbreak of the First World War. They decorated it carefully, making it more homely than any of their previous apartments, and Joyce took particular pride in having his family portraits, which he had had restored in Dublin, hung there in the spring of 1913.

Connemara by Paul Henry, as Joyce would have seen it on his visit there in 1912. He also travelled offshore to the Aran Islands, immortalized by his friend J. M. Synge (Bridgeman Art Library / Phillips, The International Fine Art Auctioneers).

After his return from Dublin he accepted an invitation to give a series of ten lectures on *Hamlet* at the prestigious local cultural association, the Società di Minerva, and he later recalled these occasions in *Giacomo Joyce*:

I expound Shakespeare to docile Trieste: Hamlet, quoth I, who is most courteous to gentle and simple is rude only to Polonius. Perhaps, an embittered idealist, he can see in the parents of his beloved only grotesque attempts on the part of nature to produce her image …. Marked you that?

By now his immediate attention had turned to the writing of his first and only play, *Exiles,* which is set, significantly, in Dublin in the summer of 1912 and describes the difficulties of an exiled writer (Richard Rowan) returning to Ireland with his common-law wife and their child. After Joyce's bitter experiences in Dublin – both with *Dubliners* and with Vincent Cosgrave in 1909 – the time was now right for him to come to terms not only with the themes of exile and betrayal but also with issues involving friendship, fidelity and love that touched him very personally. In this context 'exile' not only conveys physical dislocation, but also implies emotional and spiritual estrangement as much from a partner as from a country. Joyce explored these ideas, which had highly autobiographical implications, through the four central figures of his play, beginning with a version of himself in the character of Richard Rowan, and including his wife Bertha (a version of Nora), Robert Hand (a combination of various Joyce 'betrayers', from Gogarty to Cosgrave to Prezioso, who he had taken to task for overstepping

the mark in his advances to Nora a year or so previously) and finally Beatrice (drawn at least in part from Mary Sheehy, daughter of the Dublin family he had been friendly with while still at school, and from Trieste's Amalia Popper, very probably the mystery lady who is the object of Giacomo's desires in *Giacomo Joyce*). *Exiles* centres around a meeting between Robert, Richard's old friend, and Bertha, who feels estranged from her husband and burdened by the freedom he gives her within their relationship. During what Joyce termed 'three cat-and-mouse acts', Richard asserts his belief in the need for unlimited freedom, allowing Bertha to meet Robert, but pays a heavy price for this because he suspects she betrays him with his friend and concludes that betrayal (of which he is also guilty) is inevitable.

Joyce must have proceeded with a heavy heart, however, as *Dubliners*, a work he knew had a major literary value, was still not in print. In November 1913 he decided to make one last effort to publish it and wrote to Grant Richards, who, to his surprise, agreed to read it again. Further good news arrived in an unexpected letter from the London-based American poet Ezra Pound, who in mid-December 1913, asked if he could take a look at Joyce's work with a view to publishing it in various magazines he was involved with. On receiving from Joyce a copy of *Dubliners* and the first chapter of *A Portrait of the Artist as a Young Man*, Pound declared them 'damn fine stuff' and soon convinced the English journal, *The Egoist*, which was edited by Dora Marsden and Harriet Shaw Weaver, firstly to publish 'A Curious History', Joyce's description of his efforts to publish *Dubliners*, and then *A Portrait of the Artist as a Young Man*, in fifteen-page instalments beginning in February

1914. Encouraged by Pound's praise and his practical help, Joyce felt his position strengthening and wrote demanding a decision about *Dubliners* from Grant Richards, who finally agreed, in January 1914, to publish 1,250 copies, insisting however that no royalties be paid on the first 500 and that Joyce buy 120 copies to sell in Trieste. Finally, on 15 June 1914, *Dubliners* appeared in print, receiving reasonably warm reviews and raising none of the scandal Maunsel & Co. had predicted. Joyce managed to sell most of the 120 copies to his friends in Trieste, although

Ezra Pound (1885–1972), the American critic and poet (whose most celebrated work was The Cantos*), played a vital role in helping establish Joyce in Paris and London. In 1914 he arranged for the English journal* The Egoist *to serialize Joyce's* A Portrait of the Artist as a Young Man. *Later, in 1920, he convinced Joyce to leave Trieste and settle in Paris (Weidenfeld Archive).*

Joyce looking a little like Ezra Pound (State University of New York at Buffalo).

he was disappointed to discover at the year's end that just 499 copies had been sold in total, one short of the number needed before royalties became payable.

With *Dubliners* and *A Portrait of the Artist as a Young Man* thus launched, Joyce was fully formed as an artist, and the path was clear for him to set to work on *Ulysses*, the story he had first conceived in Rome and which he later described as the 'epic of two races' (the Jewish and the Irish). *Ulysses* is primarily a book about Joyce's Dublin, a cosmopolitan city which resounds with echoes from all over Europe. The characters are all genuine Dubliners, yet Stephen Dedalus brings with him Greek elements, Leopold Bloom has a vital middle-European, Austro-Hungarian, Jewish background, and his wife Molly was born in Gibraltar, the daughter of Major Brian Tweedy and Lunita Laredo, his Spanish-Jewish wife. While Joyce took Dublin with him to Europe and treasured it for years before rendering it with extraordinary precision in his novel, he also brought to the Dublin of *Ulysses* his second city, Trieste, a southern seaport and a 'Europiccola' (to use the term given it in *Finnegans Wake*), a little Europe where, as George Eliot put it in *Daniel Deronda*, 'the garments

The Jewish Synagogue in Trieste shortly before its inauguration in 1912. In Joyce's time Trieste's Jewish population numbered about 6,000. By and large the community was rich and influential. Trieste was also temporary home to large numbers of Jews from Eastern Europe on their way to Palestine and the United States. For this reason the city was known as the Port of the Orient (Archivio Fantin).

R, Muhammad, the Bride of Lammermoor, Peter the Hermit, Peter the Packer, Dark Rosaleen, Patrick/Shakespeare,

⊥ W.

W / Jack the Giantkiller,

M / Cleopatra, Savourneen Deelish,

L / my brown son.

X

So anyhow Terry brought the three pints Joe was standing and begob the sight nearly left my eyes when I saw him land out a quid. O, as true as I'm telling you. A goodlooking sovereign.

— And there's more where that came from, says he.

— Were you robbing the poorbox, Joe? say I?

— Sweat of my brow, says Joe. 'Twas the prudent member gave me the wheeze.

— I saw him before I met you, says I, sloping around by Pill lane and Greek street with his cod's eye counting up all the guts of the fish.

Who comes through Michan's land, bedight in sable armour? O'Bloom, the son of Rory: it is he. Impervious to fear is Rory's son: he of the prudent soul.

— For the old woman of Prince's street, says the citizen, the subsidised organ. The pledgebound party on the floor of the house. And look at this blasted rag, says he. Look at this, says he. *The Irish Independent*, if you please, founded by Parnell to be the workingman's friend. Listen to the births and deaths in the *Irish all for Ireland Independent* and I'll thank you and the marriages.

And he starts reading them out:

— Gordon, Barnfield Crescent, Exeter; Redmayne of Iffley, Saint Anne's on Sea, the wife of William T. Redmayne, of a son. How's that, eh? Wright and Flint, Vincent and Gillett to Rotha Marion daughter of Rosa and the late George Alfred Gillett 179 Clapham Road, Stockwell, Playwood and Ridsdale at Saint Jude's Kensington by the very reverend Dr Forrest, Dean of Worcester, eh? Deaths. Bristow, at Whitehall lane, London: Carr, Stoke Newington of gastritis and heart disease: Cockburn, at the Moat house, Chepstow...

— I know that fellow, says Joe, from bitter experience.

— Cockburn. Dimsey, wife of David Dimsey, late of the admiralty: Miller, Tottenham, aged eightyfive: Welsh, June 12, at 35 Canning Street, Liverpool, Isabella Helen. How's that for a national press, eh? How's that for Martin Murphy, the Bantry jobber?

— Ah, well, says Joe, handing round the boose. Thanks be to God they had the start of us. Drink that, citizen.

— I will, says he, honourable person.

— Health, Joe, says I. And all down the form.

Ah! Ow! Don't be talking! I was blue mouldy for the want of that pint. Declare to God I could hear it hit the pit of my stomach with a click.

And lo, as they quaffed their cup of joy, a godlike messenger came

Thomas Cook and Son, the Bold Soldier Boy, Arrah na Pogue, Dick Turpin, Ludwig Beethoven, the Colleen Bawn, Waddler Healy, Angus the Culdee, Dolly Mount, Sidney Parade, Ben Howth, Lj

Benjamin Franklin, Napoleon Bonaparte, John L. Sullivan, Julius Caesar, Paracelsus, sir Thomas Lipton, William Tell, Michelangelo Hayes, Valentine Greatrakes, Adam and Eve, Arthur Wellesley, Boss Croker, Herodotus, Gautama Buddha, Acky Nagle, Joe Nagle, Alessandro Volta, Jeremiah O'Donovan Rossa,

*Below: The ancient Greek legend concerning Ulysses spawned Joyce's title (*Ulysses and the Sirens *by Herbert James Draper, 1909, Bridgeman Art Library/Ferens Art Gallery, Hull City Museums and Art Galleries).*

Opposite: A much annotated page from Ulysses *(Weidenfeld Archive).*

of men from all nations shone like jewels'. Joyce used the Adriatic metropolis as a source of many of the 'foreign' and especially Jewish elements which enrich the book. To complement what he knew of the Jewish situation in Ireland, he visited Trieste's synagogues (a new one was inaugurated in 1912 as one of the biggest in Europe), its Jewish shops and businesses, and from his many Jewish friends and students – a mixture of rich businessmen, irredentists, Zionists and their off-spring – he wove the character of Leopold Bloom.

Though *Ulysses* was progressing well, Joyce found himself in an increasingly difficult situation in Trieste, which was at the centre of rising tensions in Europe. The city could not have been worse placed, being prized by the Austrians, the Italians and the Slavs. On 28 June 1914 the heir to the Austrian throne, the Archduke Franz Ferdinand, and his wife Sofia were assassinated by a Bosnian student in Sarajevo. The repercussions of this atrocity were soon felt in Trieste. A few days after the assassination their bodies returned to Vienna via Trieste on what was destined to be its last important day as an Austrian imperial city. One month later war was declared. Much though Joyce tried to press on with his writing and keep these realities at a distance, his life was seriously affected by what was happening. On 17 September he received word from the *Scuola Superiore di Commercio* 'Revoltella' that he was suspended without pay until further notice, which meant he had to depend on an ever decreasing group of private students, loans from friends and a part-time position as a correspondence clerk for Schmitz's varnish factory. After five months he was reinstated to his position in the 'Revoltella', but by this time there were few students left; the city was emptying as young men were called up and entire families were leaving for safer Austrian cities or for Italy, depending on their politics. In January 1915 Stanislaus, who had never hidden his irredentist sympathies, was arrested; he would spend the rest of the war in Austrian internment camps. Joyce's sister Eileen got married in May in the cathedral of San Giusto to a Bohemian bank clerk named Frantisek Schaurek, who had been one of Joyce's students, and soon they set off for Prague because he had been called up for military service there. Now the only Joyces left in Trieste were James, Nora and the children.

Soon Italy entered the war and numerous violent anti-Italian demonstrations broke out, plunging the city into chaos. Despite the tumult around him, Joyce forged ahead with *Ulysses*, announcing in a postcard to Stannie on 16 June that 'the first episode of my new novel *Ulysses* is written'. For the moment that was about as far as he would get. As an enemy subject he was tempting fate by staying on and, in any case, his financial situation was hopeless. So, with the help of his longstanding friends Count Sordina and Baron Ralli, he managed to obtain permission to depart for neutral Switzerland and, on 27 June 1915, reluctantly left the city which had been their home for over ten years to head for the Swiss frontier.

*Joyce playing the guitar in Zurich, 1915, photographed
by his friend Ottocaro Weiss. An accomplished musician,
Joyce could play several instruments (State University
of New York at Buffalo).*

3

REFUGEES IN ZURICH

Joyce and Nora chose to settle in Zurich simply because it was the first big city they reached after crossing the Swiss border. Joyce was now twice exiled: from an Ireland about to be changed utterly by the 1916 Easter Rising and the subsequent Anglo-Irish and Civil Wars, and from Trieste, his 'second country', which would pass from Austrian to Italian hands. At least he had some familiarity with Zurich, having spent a few nights there eleven years earlier. Although Joyce missed the sea and did not like the muggy climate or *föhn* winds of Zurich, the city was a safe haven from the violent horrors being enacted in Europe and, on a smaller scale, in Ireland. As a result of the war, clean, orderly Zurich had become more interesting and

Panorama of the lake at Zurich. Joyce was known to exclaim of Zurich or 'Turricum' as he called it in Finnegans Wake*: 'What a city! A lake, a mountain and two rivers are its treasures' (*View of the Lake of Zurich with Villa Rosau *by Emanuel Labhardt, Bridgeman Art Library / Christie's Images, London).*

cosmopolitan than it might otherwise have been, and Joyce was struck by the elegance of its streets, such as the Bahnhofstrasse, and by the flurry of European languages to be heard at every turn; he also appreciated how the city was tucked around a lake and had two rivers, the Sihl and the Limmat, which echo in *Finnegans Wake* in the phrase 'Yssel that the limmat?'

Partly because he did not have a steady job, Joyce's lifestyle was irregular, but mostly he liked it that way. After leisurely mornings he spent his afternoons on correspondence, writing *Ulysses* and giving the occasional lesson. He worked on his new novel with extraordinary intensity, with the confidence of a writer who knew his own worth, with the commitment of one who knew that all else was secondary to his writing, and with almost obsessive craft – playing around with words and phrases for days on end until they were right. One day, after producing only two sentences, he was asked if he had been seeking the correct words, and he replied, 'No, I have the words already. What I am seeking is the perfect order of words in the sentences I have.'

Writing exhausted him and he was glad to be able to escape it in the evenings and at night, staying out late drinking with friends. He usually chose white wine (preferably Fendant de Sion, Vallois or Neuchâtel, as he disliked red, which he compared to beefsteak) and his favourite haunts were the Restaurant Pfauen, the Café Odeon (where Lenin used to go), and the Cabaret Voltaire, a meeting place for the Dadaists. He was also fond of the Restaurant zum Weisses Kreuz and found many a kindred soul there as it was the meeting place for the Club des Etrangers.

In the early weeks and months Joyce saw several people he had known or known of in Trieste, among them Olga and Vela Blitznakoff, daughters of the Bulgarian consul there who was married to *la Signora* Schmitz's sister, and Ottocaro Weiss, a student of political economy at the University of Zurich. Weiss and Joyce became close, went to the opera together, and often discussed *Ulysses*, literature and psycho-analysis on their long walks up the Uitliberg and Zurichberg or along the lake to Kusnacht. Many of his other companions were foreigners like himself, such as Pavlos Phokas and Paolo Ruggiero, who were both Greek, and a Pole named Czernovic. In these years Zurich was overrun by foreigners, not only financiers and businessmen, but more often refugees, deserters, spies, political agents and journalists from all over Europe. Despite the war, their lifestyle was good because, as Joyce's friend Budgen remembered, the city 'abounded in all manner of goodly merchandise', even if staples such as milk and potatoes were often hard to find.

Joyce occasionally met Edoardo Schott, once his best Triestine student and now an irredentist/socialist journalist and spy who wrote for the socialist *Il Popolo d'Italia*, which was edited by Mussolini. Schott was convinced that Joyce was involved in work similar to his own and he was not alone in believing this. Joyce himself alluded to these rumours, writing of the Dublin legend that he had enriched himself in Switzerland during the war 'by espionage work for one or both combatants'. He was

Joyce in Zurich, 1938, photographed by Carola Giedion-Welcker (Hulton Getty).

*From the same sequence by
Carola Giedion-Welcker
(Hulton Getty).*

viewed with suspicion throughout the war by Austrian spies, one of whom actually went to the trouble of taking lessons with him to extract information and came away with the conviction that he was an ardent anti-British Irish nationalist. In reality the nearest Joyce came to subterfuge was his agreeing to act as mailing intermediary for several Triestines divided by war, and in particular for his friend Mario Tripcovich, who was in Graz, and his fiancée Silvia Mordo, who was in Italy.

In the early period in Zurich Joyce had no regular source of income, although he soon assembled a group of wealthy private students, including Rudolf Goldschmidt, Victor Sax, Edmund Brauchbar and Georges Borach, all of whom were generous towards him and paid for lessons they knew they would often not be given. More substantial financial support came in June 1915 when, on Pound's and Yeats's advice, the Royal Literary Fund awarded Joyce a grant, and this was followed by a further £100 from the Civil List the following year. In 1917 Harriet Shaw Weaver, the feminist editor of *The Egoist*, began to provide him with generous patronage, and the following year John D. Rockerfeller's daughter, Edith McCormick, anonymously donated 12,000 francs to be paid on a monthly basis for one year.

But, in 1915, times were hard. No money had come in from *Dubliners*, which had sold a mere thirty-three copies during the course of the year, yet Joyce was not completely discouraged. With the assistance of his new agent in London, Pinker, and with constant advice and assistance from Pound, who was by now something of a guardian angel to him, he sought to follow up the serialization of *A Portrait of the Artist as a Young Man*, which had in the main been warmly greeted by the critics, by producing it in book form. He had, however, to suffer many disappointments from publishers, including Grant Richards, Duckworth and Secker, and even Miss Weaver's offer to bring it out under the imprint of *The Egoist Press* came to nothing when she was unable to find a printer willing to do it. Finally, in 1916, Pound suggested they try to publish it in New York, and so the manuscript was sent to a young publisher there called B. W. Huebsch, who, on hearing that Weaver was willing to take 750 copies for England, agreed to publish it. When *A Portrait of the Artist as a Young Man* finally appeared it was positively greeted by critics, who praised its originality, realism, use of dialogue and liltingly pure prose style. Pound declared that it would remain a permanent part of English literature, and H.G. Wells enthused about how he had found the technique 'startling'. Finally Joyce had received a vindication for his years of struggle and self-belief in the face of opposition which had, for so long, seemed insurmountable.

Exiles was to have an even more traumatic career. Having completed it in July 1915, Joyce could find no one willing to mount a production and even tried to interest an English actor friend he had met, Claud W. Sykes, in it. Because of the war, Zurich would have been a better place than most to produce the play, as it had

Harriet Shaw Weaver, Joyce's long suffering patron and founder of The Egoist *magazine, from which this picture is taken. She did not care for* Ulysses *(Weidenfeld Archive).*

become an important centre of theatre and opera, where Joyce was able to attend a host of plays, concerts and operas at the Stadttheater, the Tonhalle and the Pfauentheater. Partly with a view to an eventual production of *Exiles*, but also as an acknowledgement of the financial help he had received from the British govern-ment, Joyce decided to co-found with Sykes The English Players Theatre Company in the spring of 1918. Together they put on a highly successful produc-tion of Wilde's *The Importance of Being Earnest*. Joyce was business manager of the troupe, a role which he fulfilled with energy and style until he ran into difficulties with one of the actors, Henry Carr, a mem-ber of the British Consulate in Zurich. Carr had suc-cessfully played Algernon Moncrieff and was consider-ably miffed when Joyce handed him just 10 francs (the fee he gave all the amateurs) as payment for his per-formances. When he demanded reimbursement for his costume, for which he had paid 150 francs, he was met with Joyce's counter-demand for 25 francs for unpaid tickets. Later Carr accused the Irish writer of being a swindler and threatened to wring his neck; Joyce then put matters into the hands of his solicitors. What fol-lowed were two acrimonious and costly lawsuits, one of which Joyce lost, leaving him so incensed by the attitude of Carr and the officials of the British delega-tion that he started buying German newspapers. What brought them to court were petty differences, but beneath lay their contrasting views of the war. Carr was an ultra-patriotic Englishman, who was still recovering from serious injury and imprisonment, while Joyce remained studiously detached from the war and was openly fearful of violence of all sorts. Joyce later took his revenge by using his opponent as the model for the drunken and uncouth British soldier, Private Harry Carr, who attacks Stephen Dedalus in the 'Circe' episode of *Ulysses*.

The English Players went on to present a triple bill consisting of *The Twelve Pound Look* by J. M. Barrie, Synge's *Riders to the Sea* (featuring Nora as Cathleen), and

The playbill of the English Players at the Pfauentheater, Zurich, June 1918. Their production of Riders to the Sea *by J. M. Synge featured Nora Joyce as Cathleen (Weidenfeld Archive / Zurich Public Library).*

Nora and her children,
Lucia (eleven) and Giorgio
(thirteen) in 1918. Joyce
is missing — not an unusual
occurrence in their lives
(State University of New York
at Buffalo).

Shaw's *The Dark Lady of the Sonnets*, but it never fulfilled its promise to produce *Exiles*. In 1918, however, the play was finally published by Grant Richards to polite, but cool, reception. Even more disappointing reviews accompanied its first production, in German, which took place at the Münchener Theatre in Munich the following year. The first English production came much later, at the Neighborhood Playhouse in New York in 1925. Although the ideas and basic situation of *Exiles* are interesting and even daring, the play lacks the dramatic qualities Joyce majestically achieved elsewhere in his writing, especially in the Christmas dinner scene in *A Portrait of the Artist as a Young Man* and the 'Cyclops' episode in *Ulysses*.

March 1918 brought the start of the serialization of *Ulysses* in fifteen-page instalments in New York's avant-garde *Little Review*, and this continued on a monthly basis for three years, despite the fact that three of the issues were seized and burned by the United States Post Office on the grounds that they were obscene. Finally, in December 1920, publication was halted definitively by a court action, which resulted in the publishers, Margaret Anderson and Jane Heap, being fined. In London Harriet Weaver managed to publish just four episodes in *The Egoist* before being censored. Many of Joyce's supporters felt that some of the language was unnecessarily strong and some of the scenes overly explicit and tried to convince him to make changes, but he always defended his choices and later stated that 'if *Ulysses* isn't fit to read … life isn't worth living'.

The steady deterioration of Joyce's eyesight was a constant source of concern to both him and Nora (Bridgeman Art Library / Collection Martinie-Viollet).

In the autumn of 1917 the Joyces decided to winter in Locarno, hoping that the milder weather there would be easier on their health and on his eyes, which were becoming more and more problematic. It was an unhappy period. They found the city and its social life rather dull, and their stay coincided with a noticeable cooling in their relationship with Nora complaining that he would go for days on end without addressing a word to her. He, in turn, found her moody; he became distracted and attracted by a tall, beautiful German doctor with a slight limp, named Gertrude Kaempffer, who he met by chance and who was recovering from tuberculosis. He was struck by her beauty, she by his intellect. Yet Gertrude was not pleased when he told her he was in love with her and made sexual overtures. He subsequently sent her two letters – one of which contained a description of his first sexual experience as a teenager. Although she did not reply, Joyce remembered the experience later and transferred her name and her lameness to the character of Gerty MacDowell, the young girl who appears in the 'Nausicaa' episode of *Ulysses* and is the object of Bloom's erotic longings.

Back in Zurich, he enjoyed a further infatuation at the end of 1918 and the start of 1919 with a young woman called Martha Fleischmann, who lived in an apartment in the building across from his and who he wrongly believed was Jewish. Although they seldom met and probably never consummated their relationship, they did exchange a lot of correspondence and Joyce used to enjoy watching from his window as she

opened his latest letter. Their relationship came to an abrupt end in June 1919, when he received a threatening note from her lover Rudolf Hiltpold. Once again he would later draw on this experience for his writing and specifically for the epistolary relationship between Leopold Bloom and Martha Clifford in *Ulysses* (both Bloom and his creator used the same kind of Greek 'E' in their letters).

In these years Joyce appears to have largely withdrawn into his own private world of *Ulysses* and to have become almost bored with Nora, almost keen that they should both explore extra-marital fascinations. Behind all of these would-be infidelities, which probably never got beyond the preliminaries, was Joyce's need to feel at first hand the betrayal which so attracted and appalled him, and which he made so central to *Ulysses*. As Nora said, his motivation for pushing her towards other men was 'so that he will have something to write about'. Yet, when any of the men he encouraged to court her did so with any determination, he dared not see his longing carried through to its conclusion. His jealousy cut through his writerly needs and he reasserted his role as jealous husband by attacking Nora's suitors (such as Ottocaro Weiss) with a vehemence that was often excessive and unfair.

However hurt Nora was by her husband's strange behaviour, she remained constant in her attentions to him, nursing him patiently through his various illnesses. A source of concern for both of them was the continuing deterioration of his eyesight. In the autumn of 1917 he had a fierce attack of glaucoma and shortly afterwards had to undergo an iridectomy. She was also increasingly worried about the effect of his drinking on his eyes, especially after he became friendly with

Paul and August Suter, and Frank Budgen, the convivial, self-educated English artist he met in 1918 and with whom he enjoyed many a night out on the town. To a large extent Budgen assumed the role that had been Stannie's; he genuinely got to know Joyce well, became a vital source of help and encouragement to him, and was a more indulgent and practised drinking partner than Joyce's brother would ever be. Widely read in literature and philosophy, he was a shrewd critic of Joyce's literary enterprise and his *James Joyce and the Making of Ulysses* is not only the best guide to Joyce's Zurich years but also one of the most useful introductions to *Ulysses* itself.

For the first time in his life Joyce was secure financially and the second half of his stay in Zurich was more than comfortable. With regular money coming in from Miss Weaver and Mrs McCormick, some royalties from *A Portrait of the Artist as a Young Man* and advances on *Ulysses*, he finally had the living he had always felt the world owed him. 1919 was an even better year because Padraic and Mary Colum collected $1,000 for him in New York, and Weaver gave him a £5,000 war bond yielding five per cent interest per annum. But his ability to spend money – on clothes, trips to the theatre and the opera, dining out, drinking – meant that he could never receive enough, and the more generosity he was given the more he spent. Indeed, in these years it was hard not to notice Joyce and Nora, for they were famous for their stylish clothes and their extravagant tastes.

After meeting Budgen, Joyce finally had a companion with whom he could live it up more than ever before, but no matter how late he stayed out drinking, telling stories, singing songs or doing his famous 'spider

Nora on her own at the seaside (State University of New York at Buffalo).

dance', he rarely missed a day of work on his *Ulysses* and managed to complete at least thirteen episodes before leaving Zurich. His total absorption in his book, coupled with his eye problems, caused him sometimes to neglect or ignore Nora, Giorgio and Lucia, all of whom paid a price for his often silent presence and his seeming lack of interest. Like his father before him, he was a different man when out on the town and enjoyed every minute of his new status as a celebrated writer with a devoted circle of admirers.

Joyce probably did well to enjoy it all while it lasted, because with the war's end and the consequent exodus of refugees, Zurich soon lost its special atmosphere and became terribly expensive. His situation became more difficult in the summer of 1919, when Mrs McCormick stopped paying him his subsidy after he refused to yield to her pressure that he be analysed by Jung at her expense. While it is not clear why she took this decision, Joyce chose to blame his old friend Ottocaro Weiss, an acquaintance both of McCormick and of Jung, and broke with him completely. In the light of these events Joyce had no reason to stay on in Zurich and decided to return with his family to Trieste.

When they got there in mid-October 1919, Joyce found the character and atmosphere of the city changed utterly. It was no longer the entertaining workshop from which to pick and choose material for his books, but a shadow of its pre-war self, struggling to come to terms with the brutal changes brought about by having been reduced to a secondary Italian port. As accommodation was expensive and hard to find, Joyce had no choice but to share a flat with Stannie, Eileen, her husband Frantisek and their two daughters Eleonora and Bozena Berta, Ivanka the cook, and Loiska the babysitter. Although he did see old friends and students, such as Schmitz, Benco, Francini Bruni and the artist Tullio Silvestri, he had no one with whom to discuss *Ulysses*, as Stanislaus had become a different, more independent man during his internment and was no longer willing to be his brother's keeper or his whetstone. Despite these problems, Joyce genuinely tried to settle down in Trieste once more. He returned to his job at the *Scuola Superiore di Commercio* 'Revoltella', which was in the process of being turned into a university, and persevered with his writing, chiefly the 'Nausicaa' and 'Oxen of the Sun' episodes of *Ulysses*. For all this activity, it was clear that he could not develop his literary career in a city which had become a provincial outpost and so he decided to follow Ezra Pound's advice to head for Paris.

Micheal Farrell's later portrait of Joyce was inspired by the story of fellow Irish artist Patrick Tuohy, who, while painting Joyce's portrait, started talking about the poet's soul only to be interrupted by his sitter: 'Get the poet's soul out of your mind,' said Joyce, 'and see that you paint my cravat properly' (Micheal Farrell).

4

AUTUMN IN PARIS

Joyce, Nora, Giorgio and Lucia reached the French capital after stopping in Dijon and initially intended to stay just a week before journeying on to England or perhaps even Ireland, where Joyce would bring *Ulysses* to a conclusion. However, soon after arriving, with assistance from Pound and several of his Parisian acquaintances, the Joyces found themselves set up in a small apartment with borrowed furniture and rapidly lost their inclination for further adventure. They were, after all, in the great literary centre of the post-war world, among an extraordinary gathering of exiled writers and artists, including Ernest Hemingway, Djuana Barnes, Gertrude Stein, F. Scott Fitzgerald and Henry Miller, even though Joyce remained somewhat indifferent to this

The River Seine, which winds its way through Paris, is fondly recalled in Finnegans Wake *as the 'Sein annews' (The Ile de la Cité and the Palais du Louvre, Paris by Luigi Loir, Bridgeman Art Library / Fine Art Society).*

aspect of the French capital and preferred to think of it as 'the last of the human cities'.

Their early Paris apartments – and there were many – had a temporary feel to them and were rather cold and lacking in homeliness. These factors probably partially explain why Joyce himself came across in this period as rather stiff, shy and ill at ease. He clearly missed his close Zurich friends but busied himself with his work on *Ulysses*. He had little time or energy to worry about anything else, including his family, all of whom were rather out of sorts in Paris. Nora missed both Trieste and Ireland, where she took the children on holiday against Joyce's wishes at the height of the Civil War in 1922. However, her trip did not go as well as expected, their train came under gunfire, and any lingering desires she may have nurtured to return and settle there were swiftly forgotten.

Even though Paris was not particularly expensive, Joyce never seemed to have

Right: A cartoon by the American novelist F. Scott Fitzgerald depicting Joyce and his friends living the high life in Paris. Both Hemingway and Fitzgerald marvelled that Joyce could afford to do so (Private Collection).

Opposite: Ernest Hemingway declared Ulysses *'a goddam wonderful book', while Joyce admired him for being 'ready to live the life he writes about' (Weidenfeld Archive).*

enough money, particularly before Harriet Shaw Weaver gave him yet another generous gift to enable him to see *Ulysses* through to its conclusion, after which she hoped he would at least partially be able to live off his royalty earnings. Little did she know that this would never happen. His tastes were invariably beyond his means and his generosity often bordered on foolhardiness, as Hemingway's wry comments in a letter written in 1922 show: 'The report is that he and all his family are starving but you can find the whole Celtic crew of them every night in Michaud's where Binney and I can only afford to go about once a week.'

Joyce's spendthrift habits also played a major role in the collapse of his relationship with Stanislaus, who felt his brother had always taken advantage of him and who wrote, in 1922, asking him to send back £10 he had lent him two years earlier: 'Your last letter announced a further gift of £2000. You cannot be in need of £10 for two years. I am. In fact this seems to me only part and parcel of the careless indifference with which you have always acted in affairs that concerned me. I am no longer a boy.'

Joyce replied rather unpleasantly, first wondering how Stanislaus, 'living in a furnished apartment without a family', could possibly be in need of money and then letting him know that he had, in fact, received £8,500 in total from Weaver, as if to rub salt into his younger brother's wounds. Relations between them never really

Above: Publishing Ulysses *was to cost Sylvia Beach dear, both financially and emotionally (State University of New York at Buffalo).*

Opposite: Sylvia Beach with Joyce in the doorway of her bookshop, Shakespeare & Company, in Paris, 1920. She agreed to publish Ulysses *when it was rejected as unsuitable by other publishers (State University of New York at Buffalo).*

recovered, although they did meet a couple of times in Salzburg and in Zurich, following Stanislaus's marriage in 1927 to Nelly Lichtensteiger.

The writing of *Ulysses* continued to be Joyce's *raison d'être* from the time of his arrival in Paris until he finally brought it to a conclusion in October 1921. It was a mammoth task – some episodes were rewritten as many as nine times and the book as a whole had taken, as he himself explained, 'seven years of labour (diversified by eight illnesses and nineteen changes of address, from Austria to Switzerland, to Italy, to France)'. Publishing it proved equally complicated. Weaver tried and failed to do so in England, where Leonard and Virginia Woolf were among those who turned it down, while in America Huebsch and other potential publishers were discouraged from getting involved by the court ruling against *The Little Review*. Joyce did not know where to turn and things might have become desperate had he not become friendly with Sylvia Beach, the American founder and owner of the legendary Shakespeare and Company bookshop. Together they hatched a plot to publish an English language edition of *Ulysses* in France, subscribed in advance, under the imprint of Shakespeare and Company. Beach eagerly embraced the plan because she reckoned it would mean 'thousands of dollars in publicity' for her and because she genuinely believed in Joyce's genius. As it turned out, however, the only one to receive substantial income from the enterprise was Joyce, who she treated with patient and even indulgent generosity. As soon as an agreement was reached, they swung into action: proofs were produced by Maurice Darantière of Dijon and corrected by Joyce, who in the process added almost one-third to the book (despite several severe attacks of iritis). A cover in the blue of the Greek flag with white lettering was chosen, and everything was, almost miraculously, ready for publication on the author's fortieth birthday, 2 February 1922.

In a year which saw such wonderful books as Sinclair Lewis's *Babbitt*, T.S. Eliot's *The Wasteland* and Virginia Woolf's *Jacob's Room*, Joyce's dazzlingly original *Ulysses*

The prolific Irish dramatist and man of letters George Bernard Shaw was not one of Joyce's favourite literary figures. In 1909 Joyce reviewed Shaw's The Shewing up of Blanco Posnet *at the Abbey Theatre for* Il Piccolo della Sera, *writing: 'It is a sermon. Shaw is a born preacher. His lively and talkative spirit cannot stand to be subjected to the noble and bare style appropriate to modern playwriting… The art is too poor to make it convincing as drama' (Weidenfeld Archive).*

was more than a first among equals. It was the novel of the year and would become *the* novel of the twentieth century. It was hailed by the critics, led by Joyce's French sponsor Valéry Larbaud, who wrote that, with *Ulysses*, Ireland was 'making a sensational re-entrance into high European literature' and described the book as 'the vastest and most human work in Europe since Rabelais'. Joyce was finally recognized as a writer of worldwide importance for what Hemingway called his 'most goddamn wonderful book' and Eliot praised its unprecedented manipulation of the 'constant parallel between contemporaneity and antiquity'. There is no doubt that, with the advent of *Ulysses*, the novel as the nineteenth century had known it could never be the same again.

Of course this recognition came slowly and was not universal; indeed, some contemporaries were openly critical. Edmund Gosse objected to it on the grounds that Joyce had been forced to publish it in Paris because of its obscenity; Virginia Woolf snootily judged it 'underbred', the work of 'a queasy undergraduate scratching his pimples'; George Moore wondered 'how one can plow through such stuff'; and George Bernard Shaw, in his letter refusing to buy a copy, described it as 'a revolting record of a disgusting phase of civilization; but it is a truthful one'. Back in Ireland, the *Dublin Review* called it 'a fearful travesty', Joyce's father was unimpressed and declared his son a 'blackguard', while the usually sympathetic Aunt Josephine Murray was so horrified by the parts she read that she quickly gave it away.

What caused such strong reactions and why was *Ulysses* for so long considered a dirty book, 'sordidly pornographic' to quote *The Sporting Times* or, in the words of the *Sunday Express*, 'the most infamously obscene book in ancient or modern literature … with its leprous and scabrous horrors'? The occasional use of strong language, and the graphic descriptions and even celebrations of all aspects (especially the excretory and sexual) of the epic of the human body, coupled with blasphemies, certainly shocked readers. But today other aspects of this hilarious 'little story of a day (life)' stay with the reader: the transposition of the mythic Ulysses to modern times and onto the shoulders of Leopold Bloom; the marvellous compression of an age — its history, politics, religion, music, science, culture, economics — into twenty-four hours of Dublin life; the revolutionary technical and stylistic ambitions of the book, in which each episode has a distinct style, voice and point of view and yet the whole of which is one huge symphonic triumph.

Once the brouhaha surrounding the publication of *Ulysses* had died down, Joyce became preoccupied with the well-being of Giorgio and Lucia, neither of whom had settled well in Paris and both of whom were paying a heavy price for years of travelling around Europe, for their oft interrupted education and for their lack of a real home, a mother tongue and friends. Most of all they suffered because they had not received adequate sustained attention from their father, whose first fidelity was to his writing. It was hard to grow up around such an uncompromising and singular genius. But if the particular features of Joyce's nature and his genius produced wonderful, strange, complicated and at times almost unreadable writing, his children, and in particular Lucia, had no such sustaining passions to carry them through their personal crises. Having worked briefly in a Paris bank, Giorgio embarked upon a career as a singer with some success, but lacked the singlemindedness and concentration which would have allowed him to reach the top. Lucia's

According to the 'Ithaca' episode in Ulysses, *Eugen Sandow's 'Physical Strength and How to Obtain It' figures prominently in Leopold Bloom's book collection. Sandow, one of the world's most famous strongmen, gave an exhibition in Dublin in 1898 (both Hulton Getty).*

situation was even more worrying and, by the early 1920s, doctors were declaring her schizophrenic, a diagnosis Joyce always refused to accept.

Meanwhile Joyce's own health was also failing. He had to have all of his teeth removed and, worse, he was having no peace with his eyes: he was suffering from glaucoma and iritis. By November 1925 he had undergone eight operations. His letters (especially to Miss Weaver, with whom he stayed in very regular contact) provide detailed descriptions of his physical suffering and of his deteriorating eyesight, which often caused him to have to dictate or to use large charcoal pencils rather than compose directly.

I have now been put on a starvation diet by way of adding to my present pleasures. The weather here renders my cure almost impossible once an attack has set in. I am also advised to walk eight or ten kilometers a day. If I can do this with one eye sightless and the other inflamed in today's thick damp fog through the traffic of Paris on an unfed stomach I shall apply for the legion of honour.

Gradually Joyce's vision and his world were darkening. In these circumstances it is not surprising that, in March 1923, he set about writing *Finnegans Wake* – literature's book of the dark, its 'nonday diary' which aimed to portray that substantial part of human existence which is spent asleep, to reconstruct the night. To do so Joyce abandoned what he termed 'wideawake language, cutanddry grammar and goahead plot' and adopted, with moving and often hilarious results, a language based on English, but which is not language in any sense of the word – as *Finnegans Wake* has it, 'nat language at any sinse of the world'. Joyce's new language drew on an astonishing range of influences and recognized that every word was a world in itself. After years living on the Continent, skimming through up to five European newspapers on a daily basis, to-ing and fro-ing between a variety of languages, and borrowing from one while speaking in another, Joyce felt his creative powers were limited and constrained by English. Indeed, as early as 1918 he had described writing in English as 'the most ingenious torture ever devised for sins committed in previous lives'. Long an exile from home, in *Finnegans Wake* Joyce chose to be an exile from his mother tongue, removing himself from English as it is generally understood and creating from it a language grounded in English which is ever new, always difficult, and makes huge and often insurmountable demands

on the reader. He alluded to this process in the book itself when referring to 'the ideal reader suffering from an ideal insomnia', and in a letter to Nino Frank said 'for the moment there is at least one person, myself, who can understand what I am writing, I don't however guarantee that in two or three years I'll still be able to'. It seems almost as if he were doing what he described in his children's story *The Cat and the Devil*, written in 1936 for his grandson, Stephen Joyce: 'The devil mostly speaks a language called Bellysbabble which he makes up himself as he goes along'.

Joyce compared his book to 'a mountain that I tunnel into from every direction' and, in a sense, it is one the reader can never properly finish. As he put it to Miss Weaver: 'The book really has no beginning or end. It ends in the middle of a

Joyce and an unknown companion scrutinizing a manuscript or proofs. Finnegans Wake was referred to by Joyce as 'Work in Progress' during the seventeen years of its composition and he compared it to 'a mountain that I tunnel into from every direction' (Corbis-Bettmann/UPI).

sentence and begins in the middle of the same sentence.' In between, the reader encounters a mind-boggling variety of material, of myths, legends, folklore, psychology, anthropology, politics, history. His aim was to write a history of Ireland and of the world, to create an everyman based in Dublin – 'Here comes Everybody' or 'Humphrey Chimpden Earwicker' (HCE) – his head looking out over Dublin Bay in Howth, his feet in Phoenix Park, lying beside the River Liffey, which is a personification of his wife Anna Livia Plurabelle (ALP), everywoman. We also read of their two sons Shem and Shaun, who are loosely based on Joyce and Stanislaus, and of their daughter Issy. Drawing on the ballad of Finnegan's Wake, Joyce's book tells of Finnegan, a hod carrier, who falls off a ladder, breaks his skull and 'dies'. (His fall becomes the fall of man and of all men, from the heroic Napoleon to the ridiculous Humpty Dumpty.) His wake develops into a riotous party before degenerating into a brawl, during which he is hit by a barrel of whiskey and miraculously revives. Thus his wake becomes his awakening; what is finished starts again in an endless Viconian cycle: 'the seim anew. Ordovico or viricordo. Anna was, Livia is, Plurabelle's to be'. The book, too, follows a Viconian cycle through the divine, heroic, human ages before concluding with the *ricorso*.

Given the difficulty of 'Work in Progress', as Joyce called his new work throughout the seventeen years of its composition, many of his supporters became baffled and hostile as it appeared in fits and starts in various journals, such as the *Transatlantic Review and Transition*. Stanislaus described it as a 'drivelling rigmarolle', while Pound told him he could 'make nothing of it whatever'. An even more alarming reaction came in 1924, when Miss Weaver declared that she did not like his 'Wholesale Safety Pun Factory' nor his 'deliberately-entangled language system'. So shocked was Joyce by this and subsequent objections from his chief patron that he fell ill and took to his bed, only to be asked by Nora why he did not write sensible books that people could understand. Today, sixty years after its publication in 1939, scholars and readers alike admit not having fully conquered *Finnegans Wake*, even if large parts of it have been successfully explained and are enjoyed by a widening group of readers, many of whom gather like biblical exegetes in reading groups in order collectively to come to terms with the text, mindful of Joyce's comment: 'Perhaps it is insanity. One will be able to judge in a century.'

In the late 1920s, partly because of differences over *Finnegans Wake*, Joyce drifted away from old friends such as Budgen and Pound, and relations with Sylvia Beach became increasingly strained. After eleven editions of *Ulysses*, and encouraged by her great friend Adrienne Monnier, Beach began to feel she was getting a raw deal from Joyce and did not want to miss out on royalties in the event of an edition on a larger scale, which was becoming a distinct possibility. It was only at the end of 1930 – eight years after *Ulysses* was first published – that her situation was formalized on the signing of their first contract, which awarded her world-wide rights and granted Joyce an astonishingly generous 25 per cent royalty. Shortly afterwards she demanded a $25,000 pay-off in order to allow other editions and was indirectly accused by Joyce's friends of standing in his way. She promptly dropped her demand and said she would claim no more royalties. From now on their friendship would be much cooler, but at least the way was clear for a proper American edition. This was proposed by Bennet Cerf, the founder of Random House, who also succeeded in getting the American courts to lift the ban on *Ulysses,* enabling the first American edition to come out in January 1934. It was followed in 1936 by the first unsuppressed British edition, and both received vast critical and popular attention, and sold extremely well.

As Joyce continued to compose segments of 'Work in Progress' he had no difficulty in finding new supporters, even if meetings with competing egos such as

While living in Paris, Joyce met many celebrities including the American writer Gertrude Stein and the Spanish painter Pablo Picasso (Left: Picasso: Bridgeman Art Library/Harlingue-Viollet; Opposite: Portrait of Gertrude Stein *by Pierre Tal-Coat, 1935, Bridgeman Art Library/Private Collection).* © *ADAGP, Paris and DACS, London 2000*

Marcel Proust and Gertrude Stein were less than successful. Joyce was a demanding friend and was always finding chores for his companions and admirers. The Irish
writer Padraic Colum, for example, remembered receiving a sixteen-volume set of
Burton's *The Arabian Nights* from Joyce, which he was to comb for suitable material for 'Work in Progress'. As Nora aptly put it: 'If God himself came down from
Heaven that fellow would find something for him to do,' and it was true. Joyce was
like a general who marshalled a small army of supporters into combat on his behalf.
At his instigation, Auguste Morel translated *Ulysses* into French with Larbaud and
Stuart Gilbert, and other supporters saw to Italian and German translations;
Herbert Gorman published his *James Joyce: His First Forty Years* in 1924; and twelve
writers, including Samuel Beckett, Thomas McGreevy and William Carlos
Williams, collectively produced *Our Exagmination Round His Factification for
Incamination of Work in Progress* (1929), a guide to Joyce's new writing inspired, and
largely supervised by the writer himself.

In the 1930s he was close to the American writer and editor Eugene Jolas and his
wife Maria, the journalist and writer Nino Frank, the eminent critic Louis Gillet,
and the surrealist writer Philippe Soupault. He also formed friendships with the
Irish writers Padraic and Mary Colum, and with the author of the acclaimed comic
novel *The Crock of Gold*, James Stephens, who he was delighted to discover had also
been born on 2 February 1882. He was so taken with Stephens that he suggested,
in a moment of total dejection over *Finnegans Wake*, that Stephens might finish it for
him. His closest friend during the last ten years of his life was another exile, Paul
Léon. A Jew some ten years younger than Joyce, Léon had fled Russia and his pro-
fessorship of philosophy to settle in Paris, where he now worked. From 1930 on
he, more than anyone else, helped Joyce as a financial and legal advisor, a reader
and, above all, a family friend.

Joyce also proved his own loyalty and was invariably concerned when his friends
were ill, often sending them bottles of wine and always telephoning them regularly. He particularly tried to help Ettore Schmitz when the old Triestine novelist
wrote to him about how disappointed he was with the reception his new novel *La
Coscienza di Zeno* had been given in Italy. Joyce genuinely admired Svevo's work and
convinced Larbaud and Crémieux to review it. So positive were their comments
and articles that they succeeded in rousing the Italian critics, led by Montale, to
look at Svevo's work in a new, more appreciative light. Joyce was even more

*This photograph was cap-
tioned 'Three Irish Beauties'
by Joyce. It was taken in
Paris in 1929 and shows
Joyce wreathed in the
cigarette smoke of his two
companions. James Stephens
(left) was the author of* The
Charwoman's Daughter
and The Crock of Gold,
*while John Sullivan was an
Irish tenor Joyce tried hard
to promote. At one stage
Joyce considered asking
Stephens to complete*
Finnegans Wake *for him
(State University of New
York at Buffalo).*

energetic, if rather less successful, in helping the Irish tenor John Sullivan, whose voice he first heard at the Paris Opera in 1929 and judged 'incomparably the greatest human voice' he had ever heard. Sullivan was a moderately successful tenor whose persecution complex – he believed his career had been impeded by a conspiracy to help Italian singers such as Caruso and Lauri-Volpi – endeared him to Joyce, who stirred up newspaper coverage in the vain hope of relaunching his friend's career.

In 1927, partly in response to the perplexed reactions to *Finnegans Wake*, he published a book of poetry entitled *Pomes Penyeach*, which he had written over a period of some twenty years, but the slim volume received scant critical notice or acclaim.

His best poem was to come a few years later as a response to his father's death in December 1931 and to the birth in February of the following year of his first and only grandson, Stephen, son of Giorgio and his wife Helen Fleischman (following their marriage in 1930). The poem is simple and genuine and suggests a moment of forgiveness and gratitude from Joyce at the passing of his father and his generation – 'A child is sleeping, / An old man gone. / O, father forsaken, / Forgive your son!' It is also an expression of Joyce's remorse over having hedged for years and then failed to grant his father his last wish for a final meeting before he died. His guilt was all the stronger because he remained the favourite child to the end and was the sole beneficiary of the £665 John Stanislaus Joyce left in his will.

James and Nora Joyce after they finally married in a London registry office on 4 July 1931 in order to avoid inheritance problems in the event of his death. They were accompanied by their solicitor who acted as a witness (State University of New York at Buffalo).

The older Joyce grew the more his immediate family meant to him. On 4 July 1931, he married Nora in London to ensure that there would be no succession problems upon his death. By then she was an increasingly vital presence for him and even if he more than occasionally drove her to despair with his drinking and his foolish generosity, he could always win her round and probably would not have survived without her in those years. When she had to be operated on for a hysterectomy in 1929, he was so distraught that he had to be given a bed beside hers for the duration of her month-long stay in hospital. His children, meanwhile, continued to be a serious source of anxiety for him. Giorgio rather fitfully continued to pursue a singing career, having made his public debut performing Handel at a concert in the Studio Scientifique de la Voix in 1929. In 1934, along with his wife Helen (a sophisticated divorcée ten years older than him), Giorgio spent over a year in the United States and Joyce felt their absence keenly. He missed Giorgio's reassuring, sensible presence and Lucia became more difficult in his absence. Despite help from John McCormack in the United States, Giorgio's career failed to take off. Irish-Americans, in particular, had expected Joyce's son to be a broth of a boy with a thick brogue, singing Irish ballads, and were disappointed with this continental who spoke poor English. Soon after their return to France, Giorgio's relationship with Helen

Joyce with his troubled daughter Lucia in 1924. He refused to believe that she was as ill as she really was (State University of New York at Buffalo).

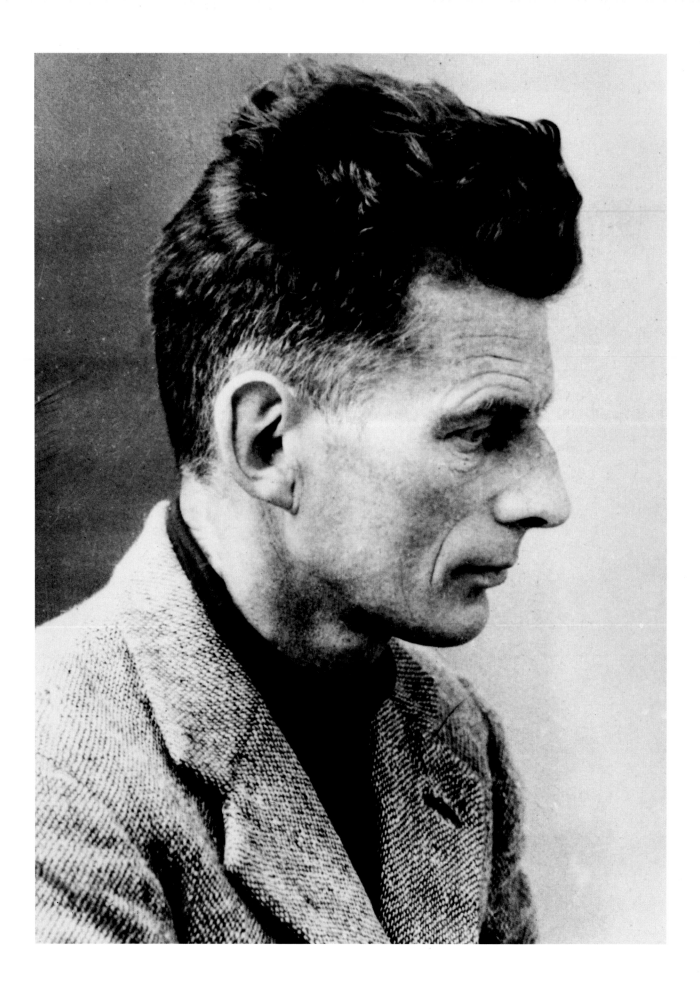

*Samuel Beckett (1906–89) first met Joyce in 1928 and for two years they were particularly close. Beckett helped Joyce in many ways, especially by taking dictation for 'Work in Progress' (*Finnegans Wake*). Beckett went on to emerge from Joyce's shadow and become one of Europe's leading playwrights with such successes as* Waiting for Godot *and* Happy Days. *He was later awarded the Nobel Prize for Literature (Hulton Getty).*

began to deteriorate and she suffered the first of several nervous breakdowns.

Lucia's case was a good deal more serious. In 1929 she underwent an unsuccessful operation for strabismus and more worryingly, abandoned her six-year-long interest in dancing. Her health worsened when her parents formalized their marriage because she saw Nora as a competitor for her father's affections. In 1932, on Joyce's birthday, she threw a chair at her mother and suffered her first major breakdown. Some of her problems derived from her unrequited infatuation, in the late 1920s, with Samuel Beckett and, as a result, her parents were angry with him because they felt he had encouraged her. He was banished from the Joyce circle entirely in 1930, after he told Lucia rather bluntly that he came to the house not to see her, but her father, and Joyce did not forgive him for many years, until eventually he took pity on him, following his stabbing in 1938.

There was little agreement in the Joyce household as to the real nature of Lucia's illness. Nora thought marriage might solve her problems; Lucia herself claimed she was sex-starved and for a time became recklessly promiscuous. Joyce felt she was suffering from nerves and an inferiority complex, while Giorgio was probably the only one to admit the seriousness of her condition. At one stage Joyce's faithful friend Paul Léon encouraged his brother-in-law, Ponisovsky, to show interest in her, and they got on well enough for him to propose to her, but the relationship, like others with the sculptor Alexander Calder and the writer Robert McAlmon, soon came to an all too predictable conclusion.

Racked with guilt over her condition, Joyce alone refused to admit she was incurable and became so obsessed with looking after her that he suffered bouts of depression himself. He was the only one to have any kind of meaningful relationship with her and, as a result, felt personally responsible for her well-being. No one else could make any sense of what she said and at times he went to extremes to justify her appalling behaviour. He spent much of the last decade of his life roaming Europe in search of a doctor capable of curing her, but sadly none of the twenty-five or so (including Jung) who took her into their care succeeded. All of this had a huge cost, and Joyce was spending well over half of his income on doctors, nurses, nursing homes, and on responding to her every whim. He thought nothing of spending 4,000 francs on a fur coat she wanted because he thought it might restore her self-esteem, or of imposing on friends such as Mrs Jolas, Mary Colum, Miss Weaver or his sister Eileen, when she expressed a desire to stay with them. Time and time again he steadfastly refused to believe their versions of how difficult it was to cope with her until finally, in 1936, following several incidents in which she disappeared and attempted suicide, he bowed to the inevitable and allowed her be put permanently in a home outside Paris where he visited her on a weekly basis.

All these family troubles provided an uneasy background to the fact that by now Joyce was quite simply the most talked-about writer in Europe and should have been enjoying the rich fruits of his strenuous years of literary labour. Instead he was financially pressed, emotionally distraught, and his new writing was being judged by many to be, as Mary Colum put it, 'outside literature'. When praise came, however, he revelled in it and was especially delighted when the Vatican's newspaper, *L'Osservatore Romano,* devoted a surprisingly positive article to him. He was even more pleased when he was the subject of articles in Ireland, for he dearly wanted to be read and understood in his native country. It was over twenty years since he had set foot in Dublin and, even if he refused to visit it for fear of somehow disrupting his chances of bringing *Finnegans Wake* to a conclusion, it remained the vital location and source of his writing.

In the 1930s Joyce lived in reasonable style in a relatively modest, typically bourgeois apartment. He and Nora spent heavily on Lucia, extravagantly on clothes and hats, and, above all, on dining out at some of Paris's best restaurants – Le Trianon and Fouquet's – and, although Joyce only nibbled at his own food, he usually insisted on paying for all present and on overtipping the waiters. As Mary Colum commented: 'Anything that deprived him of the pleasure of dining in such places, and of entertaining his friends there, was a calamity.' Apart from the periods in which he was having painful eye problems or eye operations, the rhythms of Joyce's days continued to be those established in Zurich. He got up late, worked after lunch, never drank during the day, but liked wine every evening, when he went out for dinner with family and friends. He still loved music and singing and this passion was one of the important things he continued to share with Nora. In company he sometimes liked to break into song, while his conversation was most often an understated mixture of discussions about himself, his writing and his family. Each summer the Joyces (at Nora's insistence) fled the heat of Paris and what he called 'that monotonous old gasometer, the sun' and spent a month or two on a well-earned, but expensive, holiday. Over the years they visited London regularly and also spent periods in the south of France, Brittany, Copenhagen, Belgium,

Joyce with Nora and Carola Giedion-Welcker in Lucerne in 1935. The fashion for wearing berets was set by Marlene Dietrich (who Joyce met) and he gazes at Nora approvingly. The Joyces were enthusiastic travellers (Hulton Getty).

Luxemburg and Zurich. Frequently the trips to Zurich coincided with meetings with Joyce's eye surgeon, Professor Vogt, who, in 1930, partially improved his sight and managed to maintain it despite recurring complications right until the end of his life. In lesser hands he might well have become blind.

In the late 1930s, although the Joyce circle narrowed, he was always able to count on Paul Léon, the Jolases, the Gilberts, Philippe Soupault, Jacques Mercanton and others for company and help. He enjoyed nights at the opera, the cinema or the theatre, but rarely bothered and seldom enjoyed meeting other writers. With Lucia away in a home, a certain fragile tranquillity returned to the Joyces, and he was able to bring *Finnegans Wake* to a conclusion in relative peace. He worked with incredible determination both in the afternoons and late at night, and reaped great satisfaction from his labour, even if it kept poor Nora awake at night. 'I go to bed,' she was reported as saying, 'and then that man sits in the next room and continues laughing about his own writing. And then I knock at the door, and I say, "Now Jim, stop writing or stop laughing".' After seventeen years' gestation, Joyce finally brought *Finnegans Wake* to a conclusion on 13 November 1938, and decided to have it published in time for his birthday the following year. Along with Mrs Jolas, Stuart Gilbert, and Paul Léon, he achieved the miracle of having the proofs corrected in time and received copies for 2 February 1939. The first edition came out in May of the same year.

The last years of Joyce's life were tragic. A war of unprecedented proportions loomed over and eventually was to consume Europe, and along with it Joyce's *Finnegans Wake*. His own health was declining and he was beginning to suffer from serious stomach problems. His family was in disarray, and he was also grieved when Giorgio's marriage to Helen failed definitively and she returned to the United States. His most loyal friend, Paul Léon, became another casualty of this split: Joyce broke with him after he took Helen's side and paid the price for the mistake others before him had made of coming between Joyce and his family. Joyce was also beside himself with worry over how to protect Lucia from the war. Shortly before Christmas 1939, along with Nora and their grandson Stephen, Joyce fled Paris and went to spend some time with Mrs Jolas, who had moved to Saint-Gérand-le-Puy, near Vichy. Lucia had, in the meantime, been safely transferred to a home nearby.

By now he had little or no interest in, or energy for, the literary project he had often talked about – the awakening that was to come after the *Wake*. In these months he was silent and depressed and passed the time correcting the endless misprints in the published text of *Finnegans Wake*. His world was breaking up and, in the autumn of 1940, he decided to move his family to safety in Zurich, where his old friends Paul Ruggiero, Siegfried Giedion and Edmund Brauchbar had set things up for him with the support of many prominent Zurichers, including the rector of the university and the mayor of the city.

Just a matter of weeks after settling in Zurich, in early January 1941, Joyce felt terribly unwell. It was discovered that he had a perforated duodenal ulcer. He was operated on, and for a time seemed to be recovering, so much so that Nora and Giorgio were sent home from the hospital to rest. He rapidly deteriorated on the night of 12 January and died alone at

2.15 the following morning. He was buried in the Fluntern Cemetery, Zurich, two days later without a religious ceremony. Nora spent the rest of her life in Zurich, where she died in 1951. By the end she showed that she had at least partially understood the literary accomplishment of that difficult man she had spent her life with when, in an interview, she was asked for comments on various literary acquaintances of her husband's: 'Sure if you've been married to the greatest writer in the world, you don't remember all the little fellows.'

She was probably right. Joyce's achievement is all the more astonishing if one recalls the difficult and sometimes tragic circumstances in which he wrote. Firstly, on a family scale, he lost his mother and a brother when he was still young, saw his family plunged into poverty and desperation, and later had to endure the pain of seeing his own children singularly fail to construct successful lives. He had to battle heroically simply to have his writings published and was forced to live with continuous problems with his eyesight and general health. On a public scale, he suffered decades of indifference and outright rejection in his native land, and lived through the frightening effects of authoritarianism, violence and war in both Europe and Ireland. Both these factors seriously undermined the immediate critical and financial successes of his publications: *A Portrait of the Artist as a Young Man* and *Dubliners* were swallowed up by the First World War, *FinnegansWake* by the Second. Despite all this, he somehow managed to stay focused on his artistic mission, to maintain his freedom and his integrity in order to fulfil a calling practically everyone around him doubted and which at times he alone understood.

Finnegans Wake *was finally brought to a conclusion by Joyce on 13 November 1938, in time for him to receive finished copies for his birthday in February the following year. Despite this, the last years of his life were tragic* (Portrait of James Joyce *by Harry Kernoff, Bridgeman Art Library / Phillips, The International Fine Art Auctioneers*).

Even if there are aspects of Joyce the man which are less than attractive, even if he seems to have been and was selfish and self-consumed, that was the price to be paid for his extraordinary literary achievement. In the end he, too, paid a huge price for his fidelity to his artistic vocation, and his writings are testimony to his rich understanding of humanity in all its comic and tragic mystery.

Perhaps Joyce best summed up his own life as an exile, one apart, carrying the burden of his literary genius and ambition throughout his exile on the Continent, in the Dublin voice of Anna Livia Plurabelle in *Finnegans Wake,* as the river flows out to sea, and her voice, as she reflects back over her life, slowly winds towards death and silence:

I done me best when I was let. Thinking always if I go all goes. A hundred cares, a tithe of troubles and is there one who understands me? One in a thousand of years of the nights? All me life I have been lived among them but now they are becoming lothed to me. And I am lothing their little warm tricks. And lothing their mean cosy turns. And all the greedy gushes out through their small souls. And all the lazy leaks down over their brash bodies. How small it's all! And me letting one to meself always. And lilting on all the time. I thought you were all glittering with the noblest of carriage. You're only a bumpkin. I thought you the great in all things, in guilt and in glory. You're but a puny. Home!

A bust of James Joyce on St Stephen's Green, Dublin – the passionate exile belatedly recognized in his own country. Nora, when asked to comment on her husband's literary acquaintances, responded: 'Sure if you've been married to the greatest writer in the world, you don't remember all the little fellows' (Bord Failte / Irish Tourist Board Photo / Brian Lynch).

INDEX